DELAYED 3
BUT NOT DENIED

Real People Sharing Stories About
HEALING AND GROWTH
Book 3

Compiled by
Toni Coleman Brown & Julia D. Shaw

Delayed But Not Denied 3
Real People Sharing Stories About Healing and Growth

Published by Collaborative Experience, Inc.
P.O. Box 341377
Jamaica, NY 11434

www.thecollaborativeexperience.com
collaborativeexperience@gmail.com

ISBN 978-1-7328405-2-2

Published in the United States

Book cover and Inside Layout:
Karine St-Onge
www.shinyrocketdesign.com

ACKNOWLEDGEMENT

Wow! I can hardly believe that we've completed the last book in the *Delayed But Not Denied* anthology series. God is so good! I want to take this time to thank the authors who contributed to this third and final installment in the series. My heart is full, and I can't believe this project is coming to an end. This has to be one of the best compilation book projects I have participated in. Each story is priceless. Each author is unique and special in her own right. Special thanks to my partner in good, Julia Shaw. And big thanks to Karine St-Onge of Shiny Rocket Design for her amazing design skills. Also, I could not do what I do without the most High God, so all praises to Him. Finally, I want to give all my family members a big shout-out, especially Sasha and Taylor.

Toni Coleman Brown

The *Delayed But Not Denied* book series is a labor of love for Toni and me. We believe in T.E.A.M.: "Together Everyone Achieves More." This is the mission of our company, Collaborative Experience, Inc. Sharing the stories of fifty-plus co-authors in the *Delayed But Not Denied* Series is part of our healing and growth. Thank you, Toni—together, we have made our dreams to empower others come true! I thank God for my blessings, my village of family and friends. Much love to my mom, my daughters, Asia W. (who has a chapter in this book) and Denisha, and my three beautiful grandchildren, Kamari, Destiny, and Khloe. I acknowledge, love, and appreciate all of you.

-Julia D. Shaw, AKA "Julez"

TABLE OF CONTENTS

INTRODUCTION

The one common thread that binds over forty-five aspiring writers is the Delayed But Not Denied Book Series. The contributors of all three books share a diverse tapestry of insight, which is woven together by the drive to define their own successes. They share their stories of tragedies and triumphs with the prayer that, a sentence, a paragraph or a chapter will empower others to push a bit harder and to be their authentic self.

In Delayed But Not Denied Book 3: Real People Sharing Stories About Healing and Growth, each woman's testimony lets readers to know that regardless of what you have been through you are extraordinary too!

"We are so proud of all our Co-Authors and must to give a special shout-out to Dr. LaWana Firyali Richmond! Firyali has written a chapter in all three books! We also have Co-authors who shared their life experiences in two books in the series; Maria Dowd, Kristin Vaughan Robinson, Deneen Cooper, and Julie Ann Fairley. Several of the contributors in our book series have taken the experience of being a Co-Author to the next level and have written their own single author titles," says Brown and Shaw.

The Delayed But Not Denied Book series is compiled by two publishing veterans Julia D. Shaw and Toni Coleman Brown. Together they have over forty years of book publishing and marketing experience. They have utilized their talents to form the Collaborative Experience, Inc., which is a full service multi-media and events company. Their goal with the Delayed But Not Denied Book Series has been to create a platform to support aspiring writers to tell the stories they are passionate about. The mantra of the two partners in good is, T.E.A.M. Together-Everyone-Achieves-More!

Much Love!

Passionately,
Toni Coleman Brown & Julia D. Shaw

ABOUT
Kristin Vaughan Robinson

Kristin Vaughan Robinson is an editor, writer, and content strategist with more than twenty years of experience in media, print, and digital publishing fields. Her love of writing began in high school when she attended a summer journalism workshop at Howard University, which led her to become the editor-in-chief of her high school's newspaper. She began her career as a newspaper reporter at the *Philadelphia Inquirer* and the *Palm Beach Post* before she left print for the digital space, where she focused on women's lifestyle content, books, and entertainment news. Kristin is a co-author of several books, including the second book in the *Delayed But Not Denied* anthology series and a new children's picture book, *Just Do the Right Thing*. Her work has been published in *ESSENCE*, *Black Enterprise*, *The Boston Globe*, and in other national publications and websites. Kristin has held top editorial positions at digital properties, including Essence.com, Everyday Health, and Black Entertainment Television's website, BET.com, and has appeared as an on-air guest expert, red carpet contributor, speaker, and panelist. Kristin has also regularly ghostwritten editorial content for some of the biggest names in women's health and fitness, including celebrity trainer Jillian Michaels, Denise Austin, and Joy Bauer. Most recently, Kristin has been looking for more opportunities to speak at workshops, events, and conferences about moving through grief and rebuilding after a major setback. She is a proud graduate of Howard University and holds a master's degree in journalism from the University of Maryland College Park. She lives in St. Albans, New York, with her two children.

Email:	Kristin@krisscrossmedia.com
Facebook:	Author Kristin Vaughan Robinson @authorkristinvaughanrobinson
Twitter:	@mskristinvr

LEMONADE

By Kristin Vaughan Robinson

"You can't go that weekend. You have plans," my husband, Frank, said coyly.

Puzzled, I did a quick brain shuffle, but I came up short. "I do?"

He stole a quick glimpse at his computer's Outlook calendar. "Yup," he nodded, with the flash of a smile and a gleam in his eyes. "You've got plans." I was annoyed. I started to protest. After months of coordinating plans to help my mom move into her new place in Maryland, I wondered what in the world he could possibly think was more important than that. But as I sat curled up in my familiar spot on the leather sofa in our home office, I could tell that he had something exciting cooking for me. I felt my insides flutter with anticipation and, shockingly, I let it go. Whatever it was that he had in store, it was big, and although it wouldn't be easy, I would wait until he decided to reveal it.

A few weeks later, that late-night conversation came back to me in a flash. It was yet another body blow that I had sustained since I had gotten the May 6 call that Frank, my best friend, husband of fifteen years, and the father of our two young children, had died in a car accident in Florida while on a business trip and was never coming back home. Through the heavy fog of grief that had overtaken me since that devastating day, I realized suddenly that I would never know for sure what the "plans" were that Frank had alluded to. My heart sank with disappointment at yet another future plan with Frank that I would never get to fulfill.

June 3 came and went with no fanfare and not a second thought from me. I sleepwalked right past that date—and anything and everything else that was taking place around me. To be honest, I functioned on auto-pilot. The car seemed to just point itself in the direction of our children's day camp that summer. Looking back, I realize that the routine of taking them and picking them up forced me—thankfully—to pull back the covers, pile my hair into an unkempt bun, and have a reason to leave the house each day, despite wanting to shut the world out forever. Meals found their way to the kitchen table—mostly at the hands of my mother, who had graciously pushed back her move and instead had moved in to help us function.

When we finally settled her in on Fourth of July weekend, it was the first light time that we'd had in a while. My sister and her family joined us, and we all pulled together to make Mom's first new place since we'd lost Dad nine years earlier great. Leaving New York for that holiday weekend was a great change of scenery for all of us, and it helped me to get out of my head, focus on someone else, and do something positive. That happiness didn't last, though. On our way back from watching the parade, Mom received a call that my favorite uncle, my late father's best friend, had passed away. He had struggled with pain and had withheld his terminal diagnosis so that he could attend Frank's funeral just two months earlier. Now he was gone, too.

Still, the time away had been rejuvenating enough that I was ready to start getting back to myself and pulling things back together. I came to grips with the fact that with Mom starting on her new journey, it was time for us to start on ours, too. It was truly just the three of us now, and we were finally going to be forced to decipher what that really meant. On the five-hour car ride home, I spoke with the kids and told them how things were going to be all right, but we needed to lean in and be there for each other. I told them that I felt strong enough to start sorting through Daddy's office to clear a space for me to resume working on my children's book, celebrity ghostwriting, and media relations projects. As always, they cheered me on and encouraged me to do just that. But the universe had something else in mind.

The next couple of days delivered blow after blow. I struggled with several unsettling situations, including watching an older cousin collapse right in front of me, my kids, and her grandchildren on what was supposed to be a relaxing family day at the beach. Even our goldfish died. Thankfully, my cousin recovered in a few days, but the culmination of these devastating events had already taken its toll.

My nerves were shot. I was completely and totally emotionally wrung out. At home, I cried out loud to God to have mercy on me. I begged Him to please make the pain go away. I couldn't take any more and, although I knew that no one deserved this, why did it have to be me? What had I ever done? I begged Frank to help me. I needed him. I couldn't take all this pain alone. They say: "Loved ones never go away. They walk beside us every day." If that was true—and Frank was still near and he loved me—I needed him to be there now.

I sat behind Frank's cherrywood office desk for the first time since he had died. It was piled high with alternating stacks of legal paperwork, overdue bills, unopened sympathy cards, and junk mail. The walls were caving in, and my once-positive, outgoing spirit was crushed. I sobbed deep, heavy sobs. Despite the obvious need to clear the desktop, I found myself inexplicably drawn to the top drawer of his desk. I even asked out loud: "Why am I cleaning out this drawer when this desk is such a mess?" It was a mere drop in the bucket, but I rifled through it any way, tossing a receipt here, a stack of old business cards there.

I smiled at the memory when I discovered an old Maze featuring Frankie Beverly concert ticket stub that Frank had kept from a fantastic performance we attended together for my birthday at New York City's Beacon Theater. I did the same when I found the tickets from the Beyoncé Formation World Tour at Gillette Stadium on June 3 … Wait, what? When did we go see Beyoncé? In Massachusetts? In field seating? In Row One, at that? The floodgates opened. June 3! It was now July 6, exactly two months since Frank had passed away and just over a month since this concert had taken place. Wedged into the side of the top desk drawer that I had absolutely no reason to be cleaning out had been two crisp concert tickets for the date that I had been told by Frank that I "had plans." The date had come and gone. Frank's surprise was finally revealed.

Are there coincidences? Maybe. But I don't believe in them any longer. Since Frank died, I can rattle off many, many, many signs that he sends me to show me that without a doubt he is still with me, the kids, our family, and our friends. These facts are indisputable as far as I am concerned. Important documents that were unknown have drifted out of piles of files. People and opportunities have appeared at the precise time they were needed. And signs, songs, and symbols that were so specific to our life story have presented themselves. (Once, our song, "I Found Lovin'," came on smack in the middle of the reggae set at a party the moment I entered the room. Another time, at the end of the first day of school that first fall, a stranger walked up to us at the U.S. Open and handed us free tickets to see Serena Williams' match just two days after I mentioned that I really wanted to see her play. Another time, after we arrived for Kennedy Center Space Camp, a man on an airport motorized cart tooted the horn and offered to drive us wherever we needed to go, VIP style, in the busy airport just minutes after I told our luggage-lugging daughter that no one gets a ride unless they are older or disabled.) I know that Frank led me to those tickets. I believe he wanted me to finally know what his big plans were. He wanted to remind me that he loved me and that he really was still with me, although not in the way he used to be. Instead of being comforted, all that I could do was cry and cry some more about what would have been and what was gone.

Beyoncé concert tickets were both a running joke and a source of contention between us. I had asked for (or begged) Frank to buy me Beyoncé concert tickets when Destiny's Child was on their farewell tour.

"You don't have to get me anything else," I pleaded. "They can be my birthday, Mother's Day, Christmas, and anniversary present all in one!" However, when I excitedly asked if he had gotten the tickets after they went on sale, he explained how he got on the phone line for tickets, but then he hopped off to join a conference call and then they were all gone. I never let him live it down—especially when it came up in front of friends, at which times I would typically add sarcasm, a loud sigh, and a heavy eye roll.

"Lord, she is never going to let me live this down," Frank would say, shaking his head while everyone would shrug and laugh that he was still in the doghouse. I even tried to push for tickets again when I was eight months pregnant with our son, Alex. Frank put the kibosh on that, adamant about the fact that our son would not be born at a concert. Based on information printed on the tickets, Frank had snatched up these Beyoncé Formation tickets in the days right after her show-stopping Super Bowl appearance in February 2016. He had secretly planned for months to finally make it up to me. Damn.

It was bittersweet, to say the least. Like the old adage says: "When life gives you lemons, make lemonade." Well, these lemons that life gave me were the most bitter lemons, to be sure. They were sour, pungent, and they burned mercilessly as their citric acid seeped into the open wounds of my heart.

In many ways, this quote became a metaphor for my life. It has been more than two years since I discovered those tickets, and I have been forced to figure out how to try to make sweet lemonade every day as the only parent to our beautiful son and daughter, now nine and twelve years old, respectively. They were just six and nine when their daddy, the man who made them laugh until they were breathless, left their lives forever.

These days, I am a wife without a husband. I still wear my wedding rings, and I guess I will until I no longer feel like they belong on my left hand. I still sleep on "my" side of the bed and still have a few of his favorite football jerseys and graphic tees with funny sayings on them hanging on "his" side of our walk-in closet. I also assist my sweet father-in-law, who is navigating the late years of his life without his wife and only child. In our grief, we support each other. His grandfatherly presence in the lives of the kids, in Frank's childhood home just a ten-minute ride away, fills their hearts— and his—with joy. His assistance in backing me up for school pickups and babysitting as I rip through the streets of New York helps me as I juggle an insane schedule of work, organizations, meetings, and appointments. I, in turn, have become his health advocate and proxy, making sure he tracks his medications, sees his doctors, and obtains any special services he may need, like a daughter would.

I've had to put on my big girl pants—literally, after years of eating away my hurt feelings—and deal with this new life. I had to accept that God did not put us in that car with Frank. We are still meant to go forward to accomplish what God has in store for us. Our journeys with Frank have ended on this earth, but our individual journeys have not. I had to take the advice that I had been given: "Remember to live while you have life." I had no choice. The unwavering support of our network of friends and family helped create a new sweetness of life. They stayed in contact, often daily, checking in on me, my emotional state, and the kids. They offered help and stepped in to support me in bringing up our children. They came to the house and gave Alex his first haircut when I didn't know the first thing about navigating the around-the-way barbershops. They took them with their kids to museums, ball games, and arcades, and they came to cheer them on at their school plays and performances. Whether it was teaching Alex baseball or sending Brianna to space camp (as Frank had promised her he would do one day), we regained our footing one step at a time. We also honored Frank's life and his positive and fun spirit by speaking his name, sharing hilarious stories, and holding a memorial golf tournament to raise money for Alex and Brianna's college fund and to create a scholarship in Frank's name for a young man to attend his alma mater, Hampton University.

I became a Jackie of all trades, but as overwhelming as it was, I grew confidence and strength in learning to manage the house by myself. I learned to fix things and to be no nonsense when I hired and negotiated with contractors, plumbers, electricians, technicians, and handymen. I taught myself better budgeting, learned to renegotiate our finances, and haggled over buying and selling cars. I even taught myself how to barbecue after deciding that I refuse to watch Frank's grill rust in the backyard for another season. You name it, I learned it, all while trying to stay on top of the kids' schoolwork, activities, and busy schedules.

I put my mental and emotional health and our children's priorities first over any stigma that may still exist in the Black community about going to therapy. Hell, I even went to therapy twice a week for months! We joined two family grief support centers and attended their sharing groups twice a month during the school year, and in the summer we participated in special weekend day camps and overnight bereavement camps where Brianna and Alex bonded with other kids who were just like them. These camps were such blessings to me and my children. They were free of cost, but they were priceless for the rewarding experiences they offer to grieving children and families. I can't recommend them enough to anyone who finds themselves a member of this club that no one asked to join.

The kids are my inspiration and my rocks. They are true gems, with resilience and strength beyond their years. They are doing so well in school and flourishing in their academics and activities. Bri is my S.T.E.A.M. girl. She loves making her own science experiments, is active on her debate team, and is obsessed with all things related to anime and manga. Alex is a math whiz (like Frank), a gamer, and now a little leaguer. They make me so proud and are so supportive of me and each other. Our circle is unbroken, and the three remaining members here on earth are bonded forever.

As I pondered getting back into the work world, I was blessed that an amazing and thoughtful former colleague generously called out the blue one morning and offered me a temporary position where I could work from home most days and travel to Manhattan two days a week by regional train. It has been a Godsend to go back to work to provide for my family, but to also feel like

I am myself again in a small way. I will never be the old Kristin. There is no way; that optimistic and unscathed woman is gone. Still, the new Kristin is walking upright again and discovering who I am now. I find that living with grief is like recovering from a serious injury. You may "heal," but you will always walk with a slight limp that will forever serve as a reminder of the trauma—even if you are the only one that notices it.

What is beautiful on the surface isn't always what appears. My scars are deep. Truth be told, the wounds still fester way below the surface with feelings of depression, longing, anger and resentment.

In the midst of my grief, Beyoncé dropped a stunning yet haunting visual album, *Lemonade*. In it, this bestselling, award-winning artist, wife, mother, entrepreneur, and philanthropist revealed the depths of pain that she had experienced in her marriage and life following her husband, Jay-Z's, infidelity. She went deep into her feelings and ultimately forgave him. Beyoncé made lemonade. Last year, she gave birth to twins and announced that she and Jay-Z were hitting the road for their "On the Run II" tour. This time, I was not going to miss her.

I called my Queen Bey-loving friend Kisha, who knew of Frank's surprise tickets, and asked if she was free to go. I had kindly been given a ticket credit a year earlier after I tracked down Frank's original ticket purchase. I thought we would use the credit to get new tickets and split the difference. She was in, but to my surprise, the ticket company told me that the credit was only worth $100 and had expired!

It turned out that Kisha's husband, Mike, wanted in on the fun night too, so she used my account login (which contained my generously reinstated $100 credit courtesy of the company's kind customer service rep!) to purchase three concert tickets. To my surprise, they didn't get the tickets that we discussed in the upper section of MetLife Stadium; they got us all amazing seats in the 100s section near the stage! I teared up at their generosity and at the goodness of God.

That night, a booming thunderstorm poured down on us and delayed the concert for hours, but we laughed in our plastic rain ponchos and drank warm white wine under the cover of the stadium. When Beyoncé and Jay-Z finally hit the stage, I threw off my poncho and danced like no one was watching—in a lemon-printed dress that I just happened to luck up on—and sang to the heavens, knowing that Frank was smiling down on me. While it wasn't the concert experience and weekend getaway that had been in the works in June 2016, it was magical and brought a very special moment full circle.

Life did hand us a big ol' heaping barrel of lemons, to be sure. Every day, I make the choice to find the zest in it so that I can turn those lemons into lemonade. I search for the best ones in the bunch. When I find them, I squeeze out every drop of goodness that I can and add a refreshing blend of people, experiences, and opportunities so that my family and I can still drink the sweetest lemonade that God and this life have to offer us.

―――― ABOUT ――――

Asia Maddrey

Asia Maddrey is the founder and CEO of The Lightbulb Experience, LLC, a growing brand that provides professional developmental training for teens and young adults pursuing new heights in education and entering the workforce. Asia travels to high schools, universities, community centers, and other community-based organizations to host seminars and provide workshops on interview skills, résumé writing, and goal setting, among other professional services.

Asia holds a bachelor's degree in media and communications from SUNY College at Old Westbury and a master's degree in business administration with a concentration in human resources management and a minor in marketing from Mercy College. Currently working as an HR professional, Asia is a proud member of the Society for Human Resources (SHRM) and Zeta Phi Beta Sorority, Inc.

Asia is a daughter, sister, friend, soror, and, most importantly, a woman of God growing daily. At the blessed age of twenty-seven, she aspires to impact lives, touch hearts, and travel the world. She approaches life with a positive attitude and looks at everything as a teaching moment or learning experience. Asia is happy with life and is trusting her process using everyday as another opportunity to be the best version of herself and dance like no one is watching. Life is her runway, and she will put on her heels and catwalk straight into her purpose, no matter what it takes.

Asia can be reached on any social media platform, by email, or through her website.

Website:	Thelightbulbexperience.com
Email:	info@thelightbulbexperience.com
Instagram:	@tlbexperience
Facebook:	The Lightbulb Experience, LLC

WHAT A DIFFERENCE A YEAR MAKES

By Asia Maddrey

After going back and forth in my head for weeks, I finally made a decision. I had been asking myself, "Should I end my marriage or should I not?" I struggled with the fact that I had made a commitment, and I felt stuck. I would wake up in the middle of the night, unable to control my emotions. I would spend the first few hours of most of my days holding back tears and contemplating whether I should tell my mom and let her know about the mess I had gotten myself into. One day, after semi-clearing my voice just enough to formulate a proper sentence, I broke down called her. I told her that I needed to come clean, and I needed to do it right away. She told me to meet her at the house, and I left work immediately.

That hour train ride had my mind racing. I was trying to figure out how I was going to tell my mother that I'd been married to this psycho for three months. I had no idea how I would give her all the gruesome details. To my surprise, once I got to the door, she opened it before I could even put in the key. I fell straight in her arms and started to cry. The words came blurting out. "I married him, Mom! I married him behind your and Daddy's backs!" She said, "Oh, my God, why would you do that?" I had no response, just tears. Because she had appointments to tend to that day, we got in the car. She drove and I talked. I explained everything to her on the way. I told her how I had secretly married the man that she and my father had told me not to. I wished that was the worst of it and that was all I had to fess up to, but it wasn't.

After three months of being married, I woke up one morning at four o'clock from a nightmare concerning my husband that had me feeling sick to my stomach. Something inside me told me to check his phone. I had never done this before because I'd always felt that if I was with him, I should be able to trust him. That was mistake number one. The feeling I had wouldn't let me go back to sleep, so I did it. I went through his phone and found it all. I scrolled through his texts and saw a bunch of unsaved numbers, which was a big red flag for me. Most of them were from his clients (he was a personal trainer), but it didn't take me long to find the dirt. One of the messages was from his boss's girlfriend. He was telling the woman that his boss didn't respect her and how she should leave him. In between the things he told her were other flirtatious comments, which proved to me that the man had no loyalty. His boss had been nothing but good to him. He was supportive of him and always had his back when he did stupid things, and this was how he repaid him.

The next set of texts was from a woman who lived only a few miles away but had always professed her love for him. He would tell her that he was in a relationship but then turn around and ask her if she enjoyed sucking d**k. If that wasn't enough, he had to take it to a whole new level by texting with a trans man. This man was a longtime female friend of his that lived her life as a man, referring to herself using male pronouns, someone you could barely even tell was a woman at all. To make the plot even thicker, she was married to another woman. He would talk to her about the things he wanted "him" to do to him. And he would ask my husband for money. My husband responded that as long as he was willing to perform some very graphic and specific sexual favors, he would oblige.

I told my mother that I almost went to jail that night because of the way I beat him out of his sleep. I picked up everything I could find, even my six-headed lamp, and swung at him. You would have thought I was a professional baseball player by the way I swung that lamp. My mom was shocked and disappointed, to say the least. She had told me before to leave him alone. Both she and my father had told me that he wasn't the man who was supposed to be my husband. This man had serious mental and emotional issues, but I felt that if you love someone, you should stick it out. I tried to help him through his issues and extremes, just to have someone around that I thought truly loved me for once. I had to find out the hard way that they were right. It was painful to admit that I had allowed myself to go through so much over the past year with such an emotionally and mentally unstable man. To turn around and find out that my husband was getting f**k*d by another woman's husband with a plastic d**k was just too much.

After I cried for a few minutes more, my mother turned to me and told me that I had to tell my father. At that point, the tears fell even harder. I didn't want to tell my dad what I had done. He was barely speaking to me, thinking that I was just "engaged" to this fool. My father was pissed because he didn't ask him for my hand in marriage, even after I told him that he had to at least do that. Thinking back on it, I was stupid for marrying him in the first place. This man has known my family most of our lives and didn't give my father the respect of asking for his daughter's hand like a man. My father used to drive us to middle school together. He even slept in my house as a child. Our parents were damn near best friends, and he couldn't even show respect to someone that wasn't even a stranger. I should have known. Guys like him don't know how to show respect or look a real man in the eyes because it reminds them of how much of a man they aren't or how they have to pretend to be one. I was so mad at myself because my father has always been my best friend and I let what I forced myself to believe was love get in the way of the relationship I had with him, the one man who truly loves me. I had disrespected my dad by marrying a scumbag, and I was dead wrong.

My father is a very calm and collected guy, so when I told him, he just shook his head and said, "Well, Asia, you're grown, you made a f**k*d-up decision, and now you have to deal with it." I know this might sound cold, but I saw the disappointment on my father's face. He's not a pity-party kind of person. He's a pick-yourself-up-and-do-what-you-gotta-do kind of guy. Whenever I would mess up, his famous line was, "You gotta handle your business, Asia; you're not handling your business." And with this mess, I wasn't handling my business.

It was a foul situation that I knew I had to get out of. But how was I going to get out now when I had a certificate with a new last name on it? I had this stupid-ass ring, and almost everyone I knew thought I was "engaged" and happy when I was really miserable. I was losing weight, I was depressed, and I became suicidal. I was twenty-six and felt life was over. I was convinced that I had ruined my life, but I prayed. I've always had this fear of God in me, so I couldn't disrespect God by taking away the precious life that he gave me. I knew that he had seen me through storms in the past and that he could see me through this one, too. I continued praying through my storm, I started going to therapy, and I sought out a divorce lawyer to get an annulment. I made that jerk pay for the annulment because I wasn't coming out of my pocket for anything. I didn't ruin this. He did!

The only downside is that I had to see him through the process, getting the money, and signing the papers. The process was like pulling teeth. This man couldn't find his ID or any of his documents necessary to get our annulment papers straight. He was like a child through our whole year-and-three-month relationship. A year dating and three months of marriage doesn't seem like a long time, but marriage is a whole other ball game. It was definitely not the same as regular dating. During that time, I felt like I was in it by myself. I wasn't his wife. I was his husband. I took care of him. I made him feel safe and protected. I held us down. We used my car, and he almost moved into my apartment. I had a degree, a good job, an apartment, a car, and a 401k, and I SETTLED. I settled because I felt that I had it all. I had everything I wanted and had worked hard for, and the one thing I was missing was love. I wanted to be loved and in love, and somehow this fool came around as a friend wanting all the things I wanted. Against my better judgment, I let him unpack all his shit into my life and make my life shittier than it ever had to be. I thought it was a fairy tale. I had known him most of my life, and here he was, back out of nowhere like Prince Charming when he was nothing more than a bum. If I'm even more honest, I never really loved him. I forced myself to love him so I could have that narrative and have my happily ever after, but that turned out terribly.

The annulment process lasted about five months, and during that time, I kept myself busy. I enrolled in a one-year accelerated master's degree program. I invested in my dreams, which included starting my own LLC that I'd been sitting on for three years, and I focused. I focused on what mattered most in my life: God, family, health, dreams, and my own issues. Dealing with this man made me realize that I had a lot of unresolved issues that I had to work out, but it also reminded me of something else: when the devil can't break you, he'll distract you. I was easily distracted, but I quickly regained my focus and I remembered that I am unbreakable, I am resilient, and I am unstoppable.

In just one year, I started on a new career journey doing something I love and know I'm built for. I earned my MBA in human resources management and marketing, and I've become the CEO and founder of The Lightbulb Experience, LLC, where I do professional development training for teens and young adults, aiding them in their career goals and enhancing their résumés and overall business acumen with my years of experience in the corporate sector. On my last birthday, I went to my mom and I cried in her arms because I was so happy. I was happy because I was no longer in that place of pain, stupidity, or overall darkness. I now can look back at that time in my life as just a memory and a life lesson. Am I 100% healed? In all honesty, no. But I'm way better than I was. I'm happier and focused on healing and loving ME the right way.

I can tell anyone reading my story to always remember that what's for you is for you. When it's time, whatever you want will come, and it won't come with a load of pain and confusion. You won't have to compromise who you are, what you love, and what you're meant to be. We all must focus on our own aspirations and prepare ourselves for our blessings. Always be the best version of yourself. WAIT on God. LOVE yourself, and remember in just a year what's currently keeping you down could be just a memory and nothing will be the same.

-Asia Maddrey

ABOUT

Asia Williams

While Asia was reluctant to share her story, she knows that her transparency has the potential to help millions of children and adults who are going through the same situation.

As an educator, Asia wants her students to not only take advantage of the education that they are receiving, she wants them to be good people. She instills that same way of thinking in her son, who is currently a freshman at Howard University, and her daughter, who has begun kindergarten.

As an English teacher turned assistant principal for the NYC Department of Education, Asia has dedicated fifteen years of her life to ensuring that her students receive a quality education.

Twitter: @awillteach

DADDY'S LITTLE GIRL

By Asia Williams

On the outside, I overcame the odds, but on the inside, I am a statistic. On the outside, I've been successful in my career by working my way from being an English teacher to a dean of students and then to an assistant principal. On the inside, I battle with being the child of an incarcerated father. I have been lucky enough to have supportive men in my life, but nothing can take the place of your father. I know that he is around and that he does love me, but there are obstacles that get in the way of that.

In spite of the circumstances, I have been able to build a positive relationship with my father over the years—which, in my opinion, makes the void of his physical presence hurt all the more when he is snatched right out from under me. It's like a wound that is healing up nicely, and then someone comes and constantly stabs the wound with a knife! Just when you think that you will heal emotionally and work your way through the hurt by building a relationship with your father, the devil plays a cruel trick on you and decides to keep you broken. That's the perfect word: broken! How can a broken woman be a good person, friend, wife, mother, and educator? I have come to the realization that the children of incarcerated parents are shattered and broken, yet often overlooked.

My way of dealing with being broken is to pretend not to be broken. It sounds like the perfect way to deal with it, right? The only thing about that is it takes just the slightest thing to trigger reality and send my emotions into a state of crisis. This particular day, the trigger was hiding in a pile of books that caught my attention when I was at work. An image of Elmo from the famous *Sesame Street* caught my eye. Naturally, I stopped and picked up the information packet to see what it was about. I read the title: "Little Children, Big Challenges: Incarceration." At that moment, my body froze and a slight tear came to my eye. I opened up the pamphlet; a book and a DVD were inside. And you know what happened next—the floodgates opened and I began to cry hysterically, sending myself into crisis mode.

I mean, you would think that I'd react differently since my father was a free man and I was once again rebuilding a broken relationship, but the memories of letters and drawings that I had exchanged with my own father over the years kept me in crisis mode. I didn't realize I was having a crisis until I heard my principal's voice blaring over the walkie-talkie, "SA (Student Advisor) Williams, pick up!" So many thoughts rushed through my mind. Do they see me on the camera crying? How will I respond to this radio call and not sound like a big crybaby to my administrative team and to our School Safety Agents? The only thing I thought to do was take the pamphlet and run! I ran and didn't stop until I arrived at room 202, the women's restroom on the second floor. I slammed the door of the stall and read the entire booklet, ignoring the radio calls to my attention and hoping my partner would respond to my principal on my behalf. I needed this moment. I deserved this moment to feel—to feel the hurt that I had tried to keep bottled up since I was in the first grade. This was the first time that I was aware I was having a crisis, and I needed to live in that moment.

Inside the packet was a storybook in both English and Spanish for parents or caregivers to read to their children to help them somewhat understand what is happening and why a person they love is incarcerated. The illustrations that accompanied the story were Muppets that looked like members of Sesame Street. Another booklet, a guide to support parents and caregivers, explained ways to help children cope with this big challenge. This packet was ingenious. It provided help for children who may experience difficulty understanding that someone they love is incarcerated. This packet made me realize something else. The reality is that children like me have to learn how to mend their broken hearts. I also realized that someone wants to shed light on the children involved in these situations. How do we cope?

While I was excited that we now have a voice, I had to allow myself to feel. By doing so, I began to feel mentally and emotionally weak. That feeling of weakness made me automatically go into my training on how to deal with a student in crisis. I needed a change of environment. I had to get out of the bathroom!

I immediately wiped my face, trying to hide all evidence of my emotional breakdown from my colleagues. I mean, what would I say? I'm crying because of all the hurt, anger, disappointment, loneliness, and feelings of distrust I have experienced throughout my life because of my father being incarcerated? The next question would be, "Oh, is your dad in jail? I had no idea!" And, of course, I would have to reply no because at that moment, he wasn't. He was in Florida, free as a bird. He had actually walked me down the aisle at my wedding a year prior. How would I look saying, "I'm upset because I finally let myself feel"? I paused for a moment. I said to myself, and then out loud in the mirror, "You are Mi Refined Asia, not Asia Mya, and it is okay to feel. It is okay. It is okay!" Mi Refined Asia was the name I was given at birth, and Asia Mya was what I changed it to as an adult to avoid questions and judgment of a name that was not common, a name derived from my parents being a part of the Nation of Islam. As I repeated this to myself, of course, a teacher came into the restroom. I held my head up high, chest out, said good afternoon, and walked my way to my assistant principal at the time, Ms. Cain, and asked if my principal still needed me. She asked me if I was okay. I said, "I will be, Ms. Cain, thanks for asking" with a smile on my face.

The smile may confuse many, but it represented that I had survived feeling something that I avoided at all costs for most of my life. I love my dad, and in spite of his choices, he is an amazing person with a great heart, but it was now time to deal with the hurt. I began to share with my father some of my feelings of hurt while trying not to hurt him, but I had to. I had to be honest with him and myself in order to heal. He became an active member of my family, building a relationship not only with me but with my children and my husband, who had lost his dad a few years prior. The father figure that I had yearned for was finally here! The road to feeling amazing, here I come...or so I thought!

For some reason, one that God had not revealed to me, my dad was snatched from me yet again by a poor choice that he'd made. On Christmas Eve, I sat in the car in front of my house as I spoke to him on the phone. He was out of the country making preparations to head to New York for the holidays. He always managed to put a smile on my face. Just thinking of the excitement that would take over my house by having him there for Christmas filled my heart with joy. As our phone call ended, we shared how much we loved each other before we hung up. After our phone call, I snapped a picture of my daughter and sent it to him.

I had no idea that on Christmas Day I would get a text message from my sister saying that my father had been arrested again. My body felt paralyzed as I looked at the message notification across my screen. I opened up the text message, and as I read the details I felt a sharp knife blade once again cut open the wound that was healing ever so nicely. I was proud that I did not immediately go right into crisis mode because showing emotion is for the weak, or so I thought. Here I was, reverting back to the same way of thinking that had been damaging to many relationships throughout my life. I showed no emotion and pretended to be "strong."

I had always said to him—and to myself—that if this happened again, I was done with him. He would be on his own! Except this time, my family was emotionally invested in the relationships that we were building with him. This time, I would have to explain the situation to my seventeen-year-old son and four-year-old daughter who had fallen in love with "Pop-Pop." My son had a lot of questions that I wasn't mentally ready to answer, but I had to do whatever necessary to help him deal with what was going on in a healthy manner. Based on the questions he asked and his responses to my questions, I could tell he understood. I needed him to know that this in no way reflected who he is and that no matter where in the world his grandfather was, his love for him would never change. This was part of the same speech my grandmother had given to me when this happened before. My baby girl, on the other hand… I couldn't bring myself to explain it to her. I just had to reconcile with myself that I was not going to tell her the truth about Pop-Pop. I told her that he was at his house far away and that we would need to take an airplane to visit him.

When I spoke to my dad, I had to make him promise to call her to tell her bedtime stories, the way he did when he visited. She would pick an animal, usually a unicorn, along with a color of choice, and he would create these whimsical stories that covered love and family and expressed how special she was to him. She adores him, and knowing that he will be absent temporarily, missing birthdays, holidays, and other milestones, literally broke my heart. She, like me when I was just a young girl, had no idea what was happening around her. I considered her lucky in the sense that at this moment she was not experiencing the hurt and anger that I was feeling. However, when she realizes it—oh, baby, that hurt will hit her like a ton of bricks. Naturally, I want to protect my children from the hurt that I was ever so used to experiencing, but this is life, and one day she will have to come to grips with not being able to experience Pop-Pop the way she has been used to and adjust to phone calls only. As of now, she won't be able to experience Pop-Pop until she is about thirteen years old.

I have placed a picture of my father and my daughter in a frame on her dresser that she can look at always. She and I will cherish the day Pop-Pop took her to Toys R Us, which no longer exists, and she was able to pick out the Baby Alive Doll she had constantly asked him to buy for her. I have that video to show her when she gets older, and we can smile at her excitement. We pulled into a shopping center parking lot and she asked me, "Mommy is this Home Depot?" My husband retorted, "What do you know about Home Depot?" She said, "I went to Home Depot with Pop-Pop." My husband and I chuckled. It warmed my heart to know she has that memory. I know it sounds like I am speaking about someone who has passed away, but incarceration, like death, is also a form of trauma for the family. It is loss. It is hurt. It is heartbreak.

I try not to think about the birthdays, graduations, the births of my children, holidays, and regular days that I needed my dad to tell me it will be okay in the face of adversity. I have gone through a range of emotions, starting with being angry with him, angry with my mother for choosing him as my father, and then with myself for caring. But how can you not care? How can you not care about someone you love with every fiber of your being? How can you not care about someone your children love and adore?

Many people often forget about us, the children of the men and women who are incarcerated all over the country. I am here to tell you that we are here and we need support, too. The hurt can be more than one can bear at times, so we mask it and hide it from the world. But I have learned in my older age that it is okay to show that you are hurting. That doesn't make you weak. Cry, feel the emotion, wipe your face, and never be afraid to express or show your hurt. Choosing not to talk about it doesn't make it any less real. Talking to others who have experienced the same type of trauma or love can actually help heal your wounds.

One thing I know for certain: my happiness may be delayed, but it is not denied. My family is everything, and I am healing myself to be a better person, to make myself happy. I have learned that people make poor choices, but that does not mean they love you any less.

ABOUT
Julie Ann Fairley

Julie Ann Fairley is an elementary school teacher in the New York City Public School System. She is an author of *Coco, Rainbow, Cherry, Mango Flavors for Friend*, a short story and poetry book for children. She also just completed her first book of poetry for adults, titled *"I'll Let You Know."* She is currently working on a card line for children that addresses their various concerns. As a writer, Julie Ann feels the need to expose herself and become the voice of young people's joy, pain, and struggles. She believes that "as much as things have changed, many of the life lessons I learned as a child remain the same."

Julie Ann received her B.A. degree and an M.S. in education from Herbert H. Lehman College in the Bronx, New York. She is the mother of three daughters and her late son, and she is a lover of life and all its possibilities. As the late author J. California Cooper profoundly wrote, "The Matter Is Life…" She embraces it all!

Email: Kumpanee55@gmail.com

Facebook: Author Julie Ann Fairley

MISS TOOTSIE'S CONSTITUTION

By Julie Ann Fairley

"What did I tell you?" Mommy said. "I'm not going to say it again!" Her dark brown eyes were intense as she stared at me. She didn't blink, and she stood firm in her delivery. Each of her words stuck. At the time, I didn't know what rules were, exactly, but I did know from the look on her face and the tone of her voice that I had to listen. Most importantly, I knew that I had to do exactly as I was told or bear the consequences. Ma said that I'd better not go against her "constitution," whatever that meant. All in all, for me it simply boiled down to, I'd better listen!

She spewed commands and questions throughout my childhood. I'd heard most of her "constitution" by the time I was twelve years old. Lots of it was laced in profanity for emphasis. There were always amendments: at home, outside, or generally speaking. One thing for sure, that "constitution" of Mommy's grew.

Tootsie's Constitution, I learned, was the law that governed our household. It was as follows:

* When I tell you to do something, do it! Don't ask me why, just do what I say. I am NOT your friend, I'm your mother, and I don't play with children. Don't slam no doors, don't stomp your feet or suck your teeth.

* Don't you ever let me hear you call a grown-up by their first name. To you, they're Miss So-and-So or Mr. So-and-So.

* You'd better not take anything, ANYTHING, from strangers! And if anyone wants to give you something, you must come ask me first.

* Don't go ANYWHERE with anybody unless I "sanction" it. (Sanction was another word that I interpreted as "you'd better listen!")

* I'd better not EVER hear that you were out in the street cursing or talking back to ANYBODY grown. If you have a problem with a grown-up, you come get me. Keep your mouth shut! Once you start talking back and cursing at someone grown, you lost right there and I'm gonna tear you up! Do you understand me? Answer me, and don't shake your head.

* Don't lie to me! I don't care how bad it is, you tell me the truth. I can defend you when you tell me the truth. I will not allow you to embarrass me and make me look like a fool. Do you understand me thoroughly?

* When I'm not home, don't you open my door for a "m_____f_____in' soul"! I don't care who it is.

* I send you to school to learn, NOT to make friends. I'm not raising no jackasses! Do your schoolwork, and it better be neat. If it is sloppy, it will go in the garbage and you will do it AGAIN. Listen to your teacher. Don't grow up and be illiterate! You must get an education so you will be able to stand on your own two feet.

* When it comes to friends, you pick your own friends. Don't let ANYBODY tell you who to be friends with.

* I better not catch you sittin' up in somebody's house. When I send you out to play, you better be in that small park or in front of the house where I can find you.

* Don't get familiar with people too quickly, and stay out of other people's business.

* You're not always gonna get paid for helping somebody. When offered money, say no thank you and help them anyway.

* You'd better not steal ANYTHING! When you don't have something, damn it, you make do with what you have until you can do better. Don't begrudge somebody for having something you don't. You ain't gotta be envious of anyone! Wish people well, don't wish them harm.

* I don't care if you grow up and sell peanuts. Be the best damn peanut seller you can be.

* Value yourself and others. Don't you allow ANYBODY to walk all over you. If you don't respect me, girl, give your heart to God and your ass to me! I'm not going to repeat myself, either.

"Wowee! She's crazy." I thought. Of course, my response was the slow utterance of "Yes Ma," and I proceeded about the business of living.

The business of living at the time was also me observing my peers and listening to them. I wondered whether their mothers had "constitutions" like mine did. There was also Mommy's "Stay out of other people's business," along with" "Don't borrow anybody's clothes 'cause you'll end up losin' friendship." As far as I was concerned, I couldn't do anything. I couldn't stand her "constitution"! She was messing up my life. Then there was the "No rippin' and runnin' the streets! Stay home sometimes, and if you can't find something to do at home, you can always clean up!" Meanwhile, as I watched her when she had company once in a while, another amendment was added: "Stay out of grown-up conversations. Don't let me tell you that again…Go somewhere and sit down. Stay in a child's place." On that particular day, after sweeping the hallway floor, she motioned for me to get started with the kitchen, simply by pointing her finger in the direction down the hall.

It was seemingly never-ending. As I grew older, the amendments became more extensive. Once, my friend needed five dollars to go to the pool. Emma asked me to ask my mother and to tell her that she would give it back when her father came home. I was shocked! She knew how my mother was. Was she crazy? I told her to ask for herself. Well, she was bold and sincere, and she approached Miss Tootsie in earnest. Mommy responded by saying, "I don't loan kids money, but I'm gonna loan you this five dollars to go to the pool. You said you're gonna pay it back, and you better do just that, understand me? Don't let me have to look for you!"

Amendment…I don't want you to borrow money. In case you do, don't borrow money from anyone unless you can repay them, and keep your word!

Well, first of all, I thought Mommy would say no, but she surprised me. (Amendment…Don't underestimate people) Emma smiled, and my mother gave her a stern look and a final warning. Later that day when her father came home, she came skipping down 179th Street with the five dollars in her hand. She rang our downstairs doorbell and proceeded upstairs to repay the loan. I was relieved that she kept her word.

As I reflect on my upbringing, I see that I didn't comprehend the importance of all the verbal barriers my mother put before me. Whether I liked it or not, I had to abide by the "constitution." Unbeknownst to me, she was shaping my foundation.

Everyone who knew my mother respected and admired her. I'd often heard adults in the neighborhood saying things like, "Tootsie works hard every day, and she don't play with her kids." Or, "Tootsie don't take no sh—t!" Or, "Tootsie is a very nice woman." They were right, I came to realize. She was unwavering in her beliefs and would not tolerate any disrespect or disobedience. Very often, I got teased because my peers knew I was unable to do one thing or the other, and it was a running joke for them, especially for the fellas. "Don't ask Julie could she come back out. Right, Julie?" "Shut up," would be my response as I trudged up the block to the building before nightfall. Everybody in the neighborhood knew my truth, and I hated it!

Today, many years later, I cringe as I observe many young people, as I observe their interactions with their peers and their interactions with adults. The disrespect, the disregard for others, is appalling. Many young people feel they have the right to do and say as they please, to anyone they please. "Really?" They have no limits and no consequences for the negative choices and poor behavior they display. I've seen and heard young people curse adults out who were simply trying to reason with them. I've seen them shatter windows, kick in doors, and spit in an elder's face with no consequences. "Really?"

Older people have had their share of life's woes. Death, incest, drug abuse, incarcerated parents, no father in the home, you name it. The ills of the world have been at large. None of this gave us permission to disregard and disrespect others because our "feelings" ruled us. We felt and we thought before we acted, or we mumbled something out of earshot.

There are others who came out of households such as mine who vowed to allow their children to have "freedom" to do one thing or the other. "I'm not gonna treat my kids like my mother or father treated me!" Now, generations later, we reap the effects of those decisions and the lack of young people's accountability for their choices.

Unfortunately, society is impacted severely. Neighborhoods and schools are bombarded with "lawlessness." It is frightening! Based on this "new world order," most people cringe and walk away, shaking their heads in disbelief and disgust. The days of the community reprimanding the youth are over. However…Miss Tootsie's Constitution lives! It lives in the hearts and minds of the many who grew up during a time when children had a place. It was a place called "childhood." Therefore, their offspring now bear witness and understand why certain things were done. Of course, we didn't like the way of the elders, but it was for our own good. In the climate that we live in now, we must somehow accept that a "constitution" of some sort must be in place so that households will be made stronger, better. "Wake up, everybody!" Although she is no longer here, I say, "Thank you, Mommy" for not backing down and for loving me enough to lay a foundation that still exists. I get it.

ABOUT

Maria Dowd

Maria Dowd's mission is to energize and equip women with tools and strategies to take bolder stands for the quality of their lives.

As a motivational speaker and a catalyst for women's empowerment, Maria inspires women to be more courageous, wise, and enterprising—to design a life built upon uncompromising values, their true genius, and with clear visions of what they want and deserve. Maria's My Amazing LYFE brand of empowerment programs holistically delivers this promise.

Maria discovered her vocation in the 1990s with the creation of African American Women on Tour (AAWOT), an empowerment conference she toured for thirteen years, touching the lives of more than 29,000 women worldwide. Maria later became a successful network marketing consultant, representing a line of botanical body care products and leading a team of 1,100 consultants. Maria has authored three inspirational books: *Journey to Empowerment, Journey into my Brother's Soul*, and *Journey to a Blissful Life*. She is also a contributing author to the second and third books in the *Delayed But Not Denied* anthology series.

Maria's life took a dramatic turn after a divorce in 2012, which served as a "lightbulb" moment. Like so many women, Maria had fallen into the trappings of financial and toxic emotional codependency. Determined to never find herself in such a vulnerable position again, she created a holistic life map to help her through the journey of expanded self-awareness, course corrections, greater clarity, and traction.

Email:	Maria@myamazinglyfe.com
Website:	www.MyAmazingLYFE.com
	www.MyAmazingLYFEMap.com
	www.MyMoneyLYFE.com
Instagram:	maria.myamazinglyfe
Facebook:	MyAmazingLYFE
Linkedin:	mariadowd

MY AMAZING LIFE EVOLVING: PART II

By Maria Dowd

This story is not a "Maria-exclusive." Emotional and verbal undermining, harassment, and abuse are clear and present threats in the lives of many—and I'd chance to say that women, by far, are most impacted by these breaches of trust and abuses of power. It happens in both our personal and our work lives…and it sucks. It reshapes what we say and don't say, do and don't do, and who we must become to keep peace, to stay safe and secure. For me, being in an emotionally abusive relationship shaped nearly every thought and action I contemplated over the course of our eight years together— mostly impacting my relationships with my family and colleagues. Even going to the gym was problematic.

Now that I've completely crossed that bridge, I feel well anchored to calmly share my journey with the hope that it will open the eyes of the woman who may not even realize she's been walking on eggshells for far too long… or has now acknowledged that she deserves not to be terrorized, but loved, honored, and cherished unconditionally.

I realize just how reluctant I was to own what I'd dropped myself into, working overtime in my mind to diminish the impact his verbal attacks had on my well-being and dismiss the emotional scar tissue that had become a protective shield. Like others, I was quick to place emotional/verbal abuse outside of something that was real and painful. In the absence of bruising and black eyes, societies tend to minimize its impact on the human spirit. The outside world typically experiences bubbling charm and chivalry, so it's easy to wave off the probability that dehumanizing things happen behind closed doors. The bottom line is that at least one in every five women will experience some form of intimate partner violence in her lifetime, with Black women experiencing abuse at rates 35 percent higher than white women.

I learned the definition of gaslighting, "a tactic used to gain more power, makes a victim question their reality" through lying, denying, projecting, using what's near and dear as ammunition, wearing down the spirit over time, then throwing positive reinforcements (like gifts) to keep up appearances that their behavior is justified and/or harmless (Psychology Today, 1/22/17). I understood how it all happened right before my very eyes.

During his rants, I'd regularly ask why it was necessary to yell and insult me: "Why are you making THAT the issue?" I later learned that this is a textbook example, one of several tactics used to make the abused party feel like she's the "crazy," "unreasonable," or "wrong" one for not being okay with the attacks.

CHILDHOOD DAZE

My ex-husband and I both heard about or witnessed domestic violence in our immediate families as young children. The one time my biological father hit my mother with a belt buckle and slit her nostril, she packed up five-year-old me and my four-year-old brother and headed to San Diego to live with my grandparents. She never looked back.

My ex also witnessed his father's violence against his mother, who fled with her two young children when they were about the same age as my brother and me. His mother ran away with her arm in a cast. While he didn't recall much, his sister (RIP, Dear Heart) remembered many incidences of their father's violence against their mother.

This may provide a little context to the rest of my story…

By 2012, it was clear that I needed to reclaim my life. I'd relinquished authority over my well-being, and now it was time to take it back. I had a calling to fulfill, and it was either now…or now.

After an intensely tearful breakdown in a hotel restroom handicapped stall in April 2012, having just heard a renowned international speaker raise the roof in that hotel ballroom at one of her empowerment events, I felt a deep sorrow for the state of my life. I was in an abusive relationship, was working in a business that felt more like sharecropping than a joyful entrepreneurial experience, and was desperately far removed from the life's work I was commissioned for. I'd relegated my super powers to the back seat and often felt like crawling under the seat.

Something mind-boggling reared up—it was the day my eighteen-month-old grandson was bitterly referred to as "Prince Noah." That was the last straw.

These moments had become way too frequent…trying to negotiate quality time with my grandchild, who lived two hours away, while keeping my partner's feeling "taken care of." I felt constantly forced into unreasonable positions to choose—"them or him," despite my warning just weeks before his birth to never force me to choose. I should have seen it coming. Of course, I did.

This was part of the pattern of no-win situations for me. It took eight years to finally grasp and calculate the costs I'd racked up, merely to keep some level of (the appearance of) peaceful equilibrium under my roof.

I'd heard enough outbursts of negative comments about my family— my daughters, my mom…and now my grandson? I was done with those excruciating up-in-my-face moments of manufactured conflicts until I begged to just be left alone. I'd had enough of the insults and being backed into a corner without an opening to get a word in edgewise until I submitted into agreement. "I'm sorry" became a handy and effective—though only temporary—pacifier.

It was not okay to stay under these terms of engagement—walking on eggshells, especially when we were in social settings with mixed audiences. This was definitely not what a loving relationship was supposed to feel like. What I was experiencing chipped away at my vitality and my emotional fortitude. No matter the kind of abuse, no living creature is wired to endure all of this without breaking down in some way. My safety valve was to keep him or us as the center of attention. Any self-promotion was considered a "wink" to get attention from men.

By winter 2012, he had chosen to move out of my home into his own, feeling the need to be in control of his life. We divvied up the furniture and other stuff we had purchased together. Me, the bed; him, the bedding. Me, one wall hanging; him, the other. Somehow, one way or another, this was going to work. Somehow. While he may have had a clear agenda, I was feeling incredibly lost. I'd spend the night at his place, then drive home the next morning in tears, an emotional stupor, not cognizant that I'd made it home. Some would ask why I'd subject myself to this self-torture? I wasn't financially prepared for the split and felt the need to stay on his good side. While he may have felt more in control, I was spinning out and closely approaching rock bottom. I deserved far better than what I was allowing. Yet I didn't know how to navigate the rewriting of my script.

THE GASLIGHTING CONTINUED

Then, in January 2013, we were both attending a business conference in Atlanta. I paid for my own airline ticket, but we decided that I would stay in his hotel room. Attending this particular conference in the past had been incredibly dicey. It meant an entire weekend of uneasiness. My sessions and interactions were male dominated. Not once over the course of five years of attending this conference did I successfully escape his rage, either in the privacy of our hotel room or once, publicly, in front of a restaurant with girlfriends. It didn't matter. His uneasiness (and mine) would start reeling before our arrival. He held the auto-piloted opinion that I was allowing men to flirt with me. It was a no-win situation.

Because we were now officially separated, I courageously walked into the conference hotel as a free agent. I would engage in business conversations with my male colleagues, fulfilling one of the purposes of convening in the first place—to network, mentor, and be mentored. Nearing the end of the conference, I initiated a quick chat with a successful California-based distributor. He generously shared some business strategies, and I took notes. I needed to increase my profits in San Diego, and he had some pointers for me. After years of lying in wait, I was elated for this moment to pick his brain before running out to catch my flight.

The attack came in the middle of the hotel lobby. After retrieving my suitcase, I saw my colleague trying to calm him down. I didn't want to be a part of the scene in the lobby, so walked outside. He followed me out, shouting at the top of his lungs. I begged to be left alone. He was right on my heels. If I turned left, so did he. I'd turn right, and so did he. A passerby checked to see if I was okay. I wasn't, but I didn't know how he or I could save me from his rage. We arrived at the airport via tram, and I immediately went to the ticket counter to ensure I would not be seated next to him. As nature would have her way, this was the day Atlanta was totally shut down by a huge snowstorm. We had to spend the night huddled under a blanket with scores of others in the hotel lobby. It was a very long night of trying to push out of my head what had happened earlier that day.

My financial security had taken a huge downward turn. I certainly could no longer afford my $500 monthly health insurance bill. Obama-era health insurance was now in force, but I'd have to be legally separated to apply. So, after letting him know my plan, I filed.

For reasons I couldn't completely wrap my head around, I didn't have a definitive answer when my daughter asked why I had not gone ahead and filed for divorce. I knew I didn't want to be married anymore, but I was irrationally gun-shy about making that final move. Much of my life wasn't making sense at this point. I was in a zombie-like state and trying not to fight it.

A few weeks later, the Universe stepped in.

A youngish Black woman arrived at my front door. She handed me a sealed envelope. The documents inside sent me into a gray hole of numbness. I only remember feeling betrayed by her—his process server. My reaction was totally unreasonable, but that's what stood out before I came into my new reality. It was officially official. I was getting divorced.

Feelings of immense aloneness drifted in. I desperately wanted to call a sister-friend, but I didn't want to burden anyone in this moment of defeat and heartache. I didn't want anyone saying that this was the best thing that could have happened, nor did I want anyone potentially advising me to give it another try. I didn't want validation of any kind, just a shoulder to cry on… no words…just a shoulder.

I took inventory of this new reality—I was now facing divorce proceedings, closing down my business, and mounting credit card debt and past due tax obligations. On the upside, I'd started a new job (with Lisa Nichols!), moved Mom into my home, and begun getting a handle on my cash flow gaps. And I was working on recalibrating my emotional and physical well-being.

Friends and colleagues commended me for seemingly keeping it all together. My daughters stepped in. My youngest, Lauren, gave me a talking-to about pursuing the dreams I'd deferred for far too long. My eldest daughter, Janelle, sat me down and recommended I take time to heal, to breathe. "And, when you're ready, just date. That's all, Mom. Just date. Don't get hitched to anyone. Just have fun…and date 'up.'" I understood the layers of innuendo there.

While in the midst of pulling my life back together, living with my mother was bringing out the twelve-year-old girl in me. I had moved out of one financial codependent relationship and into another. The loans from my mother were piling up, while shame was taking over my sensitivities. It was becoming increasingly difficult to look my own mother in the eyes. My biggest hurdle was reconciling my financial needs with my entrepreneurial desires as I pondered full-time employment, full-time self-employment, full-time employment with a side gig, part-time employment with a side gig, and/or any combination thereof. Layered on top were heavy feelings of self-doubt. There was much to figure out within an ever-compressing timeframe. I was smack-dab in the middle of the most uncomfortable time of my life, trying to devise workable solutions that addressed the matters of my heart's desires and the reality of my sparse bank accounts. I wanted…needed…to get back into the business of women's empowerment.

In spring 2014, I started transitioning onto the dating scene. Inside my LYFE Map, I described the type of man I wanted to attract. After a touchy start, I went back and dug deeper, further asking myself what was required of me to attract a great man and for a great man to earn this great woman's affections and respect. I expanded my options to dating men of all races and outside of my hometown.

On my Love LYFE Map page, it reads:

"I've found my Divine right mate. He is kind, intelligent, loves to travel, and is peaceful, health conscious, funny, a life-long learner, self-confident, and spiritually and emotionally grounded. He understands and supports me, values monogamy, has a generous spirit, and is healthy, active, a great lover, adventuresome, thoughtful, financially independent, and committed to manifesting his legacy work. He's a wise and successful steward of his money, the environment, and his relationships; he is someone I'm able to learn from, and he treats me like the Queen that I am."

No longer will I compromise.

A couple of years later, I created a holistic life map for myself, a holistic blueprint that addressed every aspect of my life. Its creation was a breakthrough moment for me—as I began the journey of clearing away those gray clouds that encircled my soul. I saw the light of my liberation peeking through. I was done with tolerating a life rife with crazy-making. It was at this time My LYFE Map was born.

My LYFE Map became my anchor. It was the catcher of my goals and aspirations. I had started it a few months back, and it was helping me re-create a life on my own terms. I worked on it weekly, taking hard looks at all areas of my life—emotional, physical, financial, business, social, spiritual, love, and so on. I needed congruency in my life, and I now was extracting the wonders of my past into my present journey and my future.

I started reaching out—making phone calls, sending direct messages and emails—to all my sister-friends I'd not connected with in years: women I'd met through African American Women on Tour, the women's empowerment conference I once produced and toured around the United States for thirteen years, and business associates from my seven-year stint at The Warm Spirit, the self-care company I was once affiliated with. I started expanding my tribe with new friends with common values and interests. The more I reached out, the more blaringly apparent it became that I'd distanced myself from these amazing cross-sections of tribes because it was less stress and strain to not have friendships and associations outside of my marital circle.

My LYFE Map started growing arms and legs as I continued to refine and clarify my goals and became a relentless taskmaster. I also got a mentor/coach who was instrumental in encouraging me to use my story to help others in similar situations to rediscover their light and power. I wholeheartedly understood how prevalent these abuses were, as these were central themes throughout my African American Women on Tour tenure. I hadn't expected that I'd be among the ones needing uplifting.

The room wailed…

I distinctly remember one evening session with Iyanla Vanzant. She'd shared her experiences with domestic violence and had invited women in the room who needed healing to come forth. It was literally an altar call and one of the most intense moments in our conference's thirteen-year history. Scores of women, wounded by past traumas of all shapes and forms, headed to the front of the room. And then it happened…the swelling of heat, tears, a gentle swaying, and then the wails. That space became of vortex of bottled-up pain, suffering, and the all-important acknowledgment that what happened wasn't theirs to hold onto any longer. They could forgive, release, and claim their victory and liberation. And, like a shock to the nervous system, the light of redemption, reconciliation, and rejoicing lifted.

I took other radical measures to secure my road to reinvention and full recovery, including short-term gigs and expanding my social media presence. I found and hired a young yet mighty virtual assistant to help me bring to fruition the My Amazing LYFE Map program—the reinvention of the very best of African American Women on Tour with more empowering touchpoints.

My most radical move was selling my home of thirty-two years. My financial recovery warranted it, and it has been the best of all possible decisions for me. Having gone from a six-figure to a soft five-figure household income, selling was the only way to get the breathing room I needed. While such an extreme action is not for everyone, it was the absolute best move for me—to move to a bigger, more progressive city, to drastically reduce the debt I'd accrued, and, most importantly, to be close to my daughters and grandson. We all now live within a two-mile radius. Being geographically closer to my family and more involved in the life of my grandson, Noah, by now an energetic six-year-old, has added indescribable joy to my life and to that of his great-grandmother.

By the time this book is published, I will have fully launched the My Amazing LYFE Map course, a deep and powerful program designed to take women on incredible journeys to profoundly transform their own and their families' quality of life. Far too many women have been plagued by self-doubt and angst about their current circumstances and what the future might hold, and this has kept them from taking steps to improve their lives. The Amazing LYFE Map gives the courage to claim the power that deep down they always knew they had. They simply needed to be inspired to pull from it and the motivation to move into action.

One of our missions is to take a stand for human rights, socioeconomic equality, and personal fulfillment in every area of our lives. We won't stop until we're fully vested in increasing the quality and magnitude of women's vitality, self-love, contentment, and freedom to become even greater warriors dedicated to living at higher frequencies than ever before. We are renegades who refuse to recognize limitation and lack. Instead, we dare to do what's required to rock our own worlds and challenge ourselves to experience life freely and without boundaries.

My hope is that my words will strike a chord and awaken a life force within anyone who feels ready to get up, go out, and make what needs to happen happen…despite the gale winds that may stir up and test our beliefs, motivation, and resilience. Come join me and claim that amazing life of yours and…Live. Your. Freedom. Every. Day!

ABOUT

L. Renee

L. Renee is a native of Washington, DC, and has been an educator for more than seventeen years. She is founder of the Sister2Sis mentoring program, which mentors young women ages twelve to twenty-one, and serves as youth pastor at her local church. L. Renee has developed a variety of programs to increase student achievement and has created a program (Veteran Teacher Academy) to retain veteran teachers in her local county. Her passion for reading and writing led her to launch the Mahogany Minds Book Club. She also is a vocalist for The Tony Howard Motown Revue. Her purpose is to compel others to Christ through mentorship and service. She loves to travel and enjoy family and friends. Her life's mission is to start her own learning academy for nontraditional students in urban areas. She is an honors graduate of Mercer University with a B.S. in early childhood education, and she holds a master's degree from Walden University in curriculum, design, and instruction. A member of Delta Sigma Theta Sorority, Inc., she currently resides in Augusta, GA.

Email:	ladyblackwell72@gmail.com
Facebook:	Renee Edwards
Instagram:	n_spyreme

CAN YOU HEAR ME NOW?

By L. Renee

It was the day I had been dreaming of my entire life. Thousands of candles illuminated romantic shadows of our closest family and friends. My father was holding my hand tightly, and I felt myself holding my breath as the double doors opened and I saw his face waiting for me at the end of the flower-scented aisle. The video montage of us talking about how we met was coming to an end. As my favorite love song started to play, I felt pure joy.

It was finally time to marry the man who had swept me off my feet in a whirlwind romance. The man I had planned out the rest of my life with. The man who had promised to love, protect, and cherish me. The man who made me feel like the most beautiful woman in the world. The man who had chosen me.

But then why was I staring at the note on the coffee table saying that he had left me and was heading back home to his family and his ex-girlfriend? I sat there for over an hour staring at the note and blinking my eyes as my mind traveled back and forth between the fairytale wedding that I had described in detail to him many times and the reality of what this piece of paper torn from an old bill represented. I didn't know whether to laugh at this cruel joke someone was playing on me, almost waiting for someone to come out from behind a door and yell "You've just been punked!" or to cry and scream at the same time, feeling the worst devastation of my entire life. I just couldn't accept that this was happening, but the longer I stared at the note, the more the pain in my heart began to spread into every limb of my body. I slowly felt numbness take over as the tears flowed. I had no idea that day that my tears would flow every day for the next two years! I can see now that those tears represented different things on different days, but crying was the only thing I could do without thinking or having to put forth effort.

My greatest desire is to be married. I am such a romantic at heart, and I always wanted to have that one special love like my parents and grandparents. I wanted someone to be my best friend, someone to laugh with and to work with together in ministry. I wanted what I saw my parents had, regardless of what they had to go through to get their relationship to this coveted spot. I didn't know that two broken people cannot make a whole relationship work! I thought all we needed was love, and we had plenty of that. So why was the love of my life living in another state and with another woman? What had I missed in between those countless daily phone calls and trips back and forth during the wedding planning? After all, I had prayed for a Godly man who loved me, and he seemed to be that and more.

Our relationship began very quickly after an all-night conversation on a visit home to my parents. We were engaged three months later, and he sold his house and moved to my state. We were in love and saw no need to wait any longer to be together. We talked every day and night, we prayed together every morning, and we made plans for our future together in specific details. I had never met someone who seemed so compatible, from our coordinating outfits, to our desire to have more children, to our plans to create ministries together for youth and couples. We both had been groomed for ministry from a young age, and our relationship just made sense. Our plan was to get married secretly so that we could live together (without guilt) and then have a huge wedding that we had already started to plan the week after we met. But six weeks after he moved to my state, I was staring at this note saying that he was leaving me and moving back home to his family because he missed them and wasn't happy with me or the move.

I had no idea where to begin to pick up the pieces of my life, let alone the pieces of my dreams of a happily-ever-after adventure. I couldn't begin to understand how someone who did all the right things and said all the things I thought "the one" would say could just throw away the relationship without a thought for my feelings and what this breakup would do to me. I didn't know whether to feel embarrassed, angry, humiliated, or sad, but most days I felt numb. I've been blessed with longevity in my family and have not experienced many deaths in my lifetime, but this relationship ending felt like something inside me had died. I went through the motions of going to work and running errands, and I tried to grieve in private, but his torturous phone calls every few weeks were beginning to push me farther into a dark hole. He would dangle coming back and trying to work on the relationship in one conversation and then blame me for not supporting him in the next. The emotional torment kept the tears flowing and wrapped me in shame like a blanket, as I had to answer the same questions for the next six months about where he was and why we were not together. Each time, I relived the trauma of rejection again and again. I was sinking with no rescue in sight and felt like I had no strength to rebuild my life, but I see now that someone was praying for me!

I remember not being able to eat or sleep, and avoiding social situations like the plague because even the sight of couples in love was just too much to bare. It seemed like everywhere I turned people were in love, getting engaged, or getting married during the worst season of my life. I had no idea how my life could recover from this. My closest friends and family were surrounding me with concern and prayers. I needed to talk about how I was feeling often during that first year, but I knew that they were getting weary of hearing my story on repeat, so I retreated within myself. I was feeling so raw and becoming unhinged, and I had no solution for moving on or any comfort that seemed to help me deal with this life-altering moment. I continued going to church but simply went through the motions and came back home to despair, loneliness, and grief. I remember hoping that someone would stop me at church and say something to give me relief, but I think in hindsight that most people didn't really know what to say. I reached out to share my experience with a few people, but I realized that I was talking to people who could not identify with the emotional trauma I was going through. They listened and offered prayers and encouragement, but I needed a plan of action!

I didn't know where to begin or what to do to move on, despite people telling me to move on. I continued to pray through countless tears, asking God to heal my broken heart. Despite the attack on my heart, I did not want to become a bitter woman! I will admit that at first I wanted him to come back to me. I hoped that God would heal me in that way. But God, in His infinite wisdom, has a way of doing far beyond our expectations or desires! I remember hearing God's voice one night while I was sitting up, unable to sleep, and feeling like I would never be the same. He said, "I'm going to heal you through you helping someone else." I didn't want any part of that

59

healing process because I could not imagine having anything of worth left to offer anyone, especially during a time when I needed help myself. I just simply could not see beyond my current circumstances. But God was up to something! During that period of devastation, I began to meet other women who were going through some type of traumatic experience, from the loss of a child to an abusive marriage. I began to meet women who had no identity and little to no self-esteem.

Our stories were all so different, but we all had two things in common: we had suffered a deep sense of loss of self, and we had no clue about how to reclaim our lives. One day, God gave me the idea of women mentoring each other! He gave me an objective to allow women to help and heal each other by sharing experiences of triumph over tragedies! From the development of the first meeting, I began to feel alive again. I actually started looking forward to something again. I felt my soul awaken, moment by moment, because I knew firsthand how the women I was meeting needed this as much as I did. I knew how desperate I was to just be heard, without being rushed and without being judged, and now I had a divine plan to bring us together to begin the healing.

My mission was to create an environment that would allow women to share in a platform of honesty and confidentiality without any particular religious affiliation or obligation. I wasn't ashamed of my faith, but many of the women who shared with me were devout in their faith as well and often found themselves unable to tell the truth about the horror they were living in with members of the church for fear of humiliation and judgment. I didn't want the women to feel misguided judgment from past experiences with the church, so I decided to have the meetings in my home. It was a bold move, and I actually had members of my church advise against it for fear of retaliation from my leaders, but I knew that God would provide the means to create a safe environment for these hurting women.

The vision began to unfold because of the conversations with the women who were experiencing so much of the same emotions I was dealing with. We all had at least one similarity in common from the beginning, and that was we wanted to be healed. Despite our stories of pain and suffering, we all wanted to be restored. We all had hope buried underneath the tears and shame and dared to believe that our Father would come to our rescue. The first meeting consisted of twelve women who were going through varying degrees of trauma. Each woman had been selected to come to the group because of her desire to be heard and her willingness to be genuine and honest about her status. I knew how women tend to mask themselves behind makeup, titles, and careers, so I prayed for direction in choosing women who would be bold enough to face their truth and be ready to do the work of healing. The most important component of that first meeting was to allow each woman an unlimited amount of time to share. We cried with each other and for each other, and it was the first time that my tears since the breakup had a positive purpose! I did not share anything that I was going through that night. I simply listened to each woman pour out her soul and watching the relief on each of their faces as they departed my home. I see now how the most incredible thing to happen to my life in a long time was unfolding right before my eyes! Every story shared gave me insight into my own situation and helped me gather courage to face another day without feeling so alone. Although I continued to cry daily, I found myself thinking of the situations that my sisters were enduring at the same time, and it helped to soothe me in a way that I had not experienced before. The nights didn't seem so long anymore, and I was eventually able to begin resuming parts of my life that I let die along with the relationship.

After every meeting, we would set short-term goals to try and accomplish before the next gathering. This bonded us in a way that kept us accountable to healing and gave us something to look forward to other than grief. I felt my life beginning to take shape with a purpose that I never knew existed and would never have known had I not gone through my tragedy. I found myself using a wealth of wisdom that I gathered from my relationship with Christ, and my sisters were accomplishing goals by leaps and bounds! There wasn't really a formula for how to conduct meetings. We didn't elect officers, but we always ended up with honest conversation, things that the ladies hadn't dared to share before, and tears flowing—some to cleanse us from the scars of trauma and, eventually, from strength as the stories of triumph began pouring in. What began as a meeting of women who were hurt, broken, and bruised was turning into a meeting of feminine warriors who were surviving their pain one day at a time. Our group of sisters began growing by the end of the year, from twelve to more than twenty-five women! The founding members were beginning to reach out to women they encountered and invite them to the meetings. We began moving the meeting around from home to home, and each lady would volunteer to host a meeting. With every meeting,

I saw the impact of being heard in the lives of women who, like me, needed a plan to live again. The stories of victory were becoming frequent as the sisters met their goals. I felt like there was a purpose for my experience that needed to be shared with the world. As I shared my time, my listening ear, and my own story when asked, the pain inside became less and less.

Eventually, he stopped calling, and I was able to end the grief of that relationship with dignity and—most importantly—without bitterness! I won't say that life hasn't thrown me anymore trials, but Sister2Sis is a lifeline that pulled me out of a time of great depression and despair, and I wanted to share that lifeline with as many women as I could. The key to my healing was to help other women who were struggling as well. The ladies and I became covenant sisters, vowing to continue holding each other accountable for the pursuit of healing, and we remain as close as ever. After the first two years, we began hosting an annual pajama party at Christmas to pour into the lives of young women ages twelve to twenty-one.

Impacting the lives of the younger generation gave my pain an even greater purpose because I realized that pain and grief are not rites of passage for adult women but a universal theme among young women as well. I often saw myself in the young ladies and was able to pour into them in ways that weren't available to me at their age and that sealed an even greater purpose for the heartbreak. I saw how my transparency with the young ladies created an accountability with them as well. They, too, were able to find healing with their traumas and now are leading healed lives. My fairytale is still being written, but through the survival and healing of the worst season of my life, my life has more meaning than it's ever had! I have more love in my life than I ever thought possible, and it was all because God saw fit to use me through my pain. I am a living witness that you can survive heartbreak and not be a bitter soul. I am not just a survivor—I am a champion of women who help heal each other, one conversation at a time.

My gratitude toward the process of healing has increased over the years as I encounter more women who need to be heard and who don't have a current plan of action. Our sisterhood has grown over the years with the success of the founding members. We have all had to face other tragedies and trials, but I am thankful for the initial experience of pain that taught me so much about faith, resilience, and honesty. I carry the experience without the resentment, and that is the true beauty of forgiveness and healing.

ABOUT

Norma L. Brown

Norma L. Brown is a Georgia native who has traveled the United States as a military wife for more than twenty years. She has accomplished much over the years, including owning several businesses. She is the founder of Sweet Normalee's Kitchen Catering and Desserts and is known for her gourmet cakes and sweets. Norma's passion is in her writing and telling others about the Lord's healing power, His delivering grace, and being set free from every chain that may have us bound. It is her desire to have an even stronger relationship with God, putting Him first in all things. "I only want to be who God said I'm to be." Norma is a Deaconess at Greater Refuge Cathedral Church of God in Christ. She has been married for twenty-eight years to her husband, Sean Brown, and is the mother of three adult children and a grandmother of four. She is currently in the process of writing her next book, which will be published in 2019.

Email: nlbrown40@gmail.com

Facebook: nlbrown2018

MY PLANS GOD'S PURPOSE

By Norma L. Brown

It all started in 2006 when my mother, Big Mama, asked me if I wanted her house. I thought there was something strange about it; nevertheless, I ended up saying yes to her. At the time, I thought she was referring to her living will. Little did I know she had intended it for a more immediate time, right there and then. She went on to tell me she would give me the house and that all she had to do was go to her lawyer and have some papers drawn up to sign everything over to me.

As we walked across the property that day, I was completely bewildered as I tried to take in all the information. So many thoughts ran through my head that I wasn't really sure what to act on, but I knew before we proceeded any further that I had to talk it over with my husband, Scott. I knew she didn't think it was such a big deal—after all, she said it was going to be mine in her will. "And your dad would have wanted you to have it," she explained.

By the next day, I was finally able to discuss things with Scott. As I began to tell him the details, I could see the look of disbelief and aggravation that began to form on his face until he just blurted out, "No!" aggressively shaking his head at the same time for emphasis. I should have listened to him and not pushed the issue, but within a couple of months I managed to get him to agree. With Scott retiring soon, we wanted to have a place to call our own, and at the time we thought this would be a good plan for our future and for Big Mama as well. Being a military family, we always try our best to stick together. We often call ourselves the Furious Five because all we really have to depend on is each other. Scott had two years remaining before he retired from the Navy. Virginia was his last duty station, which meant that

65

we would be moving without him. It felt like he was leaving us yet again to be shipped out to sea for an extended time, but in all actuality, this was our doing. I was thirty-six years old when we packed up everything and decided to move back to Georgia in 2008. Reexamining it all, I realize just how much our decisions were based on pleasing other people. My eldest son, Jonathan, had just graduated high school and was to attend Savannah College of Art and Design in the fall. Our second child, Andrew, would be a senior at a new school, and my youngest, Lydia, would be a sophomore. Scott and I had played with the idea for about a year before we finally came to a decision. We knew deep down that this move was never in our plans but was forced onto us by others—people we loved dearly and were willing to do anything for.

After we came to our decision, not a day would go by without talking on the phone with Big Mama about renovating the house. We would discuss our plans to add on our own personal suite away from the kids and adding a mother-in-law suite for her. One day, out of nowhere, she told us we needed to go ahead and take over the house payments because the house had an adjustable-rate mortgage and the increase in her monthly payments would be over her budget. It was then we realized we were not taking on an inheritance at all, but a burdensome debt!

We decided to stick to our word and agreed to come home when we could get the time off to meet with Big Mama's lawyer. Despite the setback, we didn't think anything was wrong and believed that everyone was still on the same page about what we considered the Family Home, something we could even pass down to our children one day. Unfortunately, I never really questioned anything Big Mama said or did, so when she had come to me a few months earlier about refinancing the home for the second time, I said, "Yes, go ahead, Big Mama. It's still your house right now." I was truly naïve. Despite all the signs, we walked headlong into an enormous mortgage that should have never been. We always thought there was plenty of equity in the land and house from all the work Big Mama had done, so we believed we were making a good investment.

We finally made it home around the holidays and met with the lawyers to sign the documents and transfer the papers. When she signed over the house, we ended up with a brand-new mortgage on the home and walked away with a little money in our pockets to help with moving expenses. Our payment was $900 a month for the next five years, and Big Mama agreed upon signing the papers to pay $700 and the utilities until we moved home. Not living in the house, we paid the extra $200 monthly.

As we prepared for the move, we began to have mixed feelings about being apart for two whole years. We began to question whether this was the right thing for our marriage and children, and if we could financially afford to live in two different states. We had always talked about moving back home to Georgia, but never on these terms. Scott and I loved Big Mama, and the kids absolutely adored her, so this should have been an exciting time for us. After all, this wasn't the first time we had come home to stay with Big Mama. In between Scott's change of duty stations, we would often stay with her for several weeks at a time. Living with her wasn't anything new, but I couldn't shake the feeling that something was different this time. Maybe it was the new man that she had started a relationship with; he always seemed to be around. Well, no matter what it was, we were in way too deep to back out now.

As time moved on, everything began to proceed accordingly, from the transfer papers to my next job to the kids' withdrawal from school. Scott had managed to find a room to rent not too far from where he was stationed. Things were coming along and we were determined to make them work no matter what, or so we thought. I soon received a call from Big Mama, telling me that she had decided to buy a house and was fixing it up. The man she was seeing was planning on marrying her, and the house was for them. Part of me was happy for her, but the other part was furious. What was the reason we were sacrificing so much? Was it really just trying to keep the house in the family like she stated, or was it a way for her to give us the house payment that she no longer wanted? It was a tremendous blow to me, but I managed to keep it together and press on.

In June 2008, one week after Jonathan's graduation, we loaded a U-Haul with all of our belongings plus two vehicles in tow and were bound for Georgia. We had no idea what this new transition in life would bring, but I tried to remain positive. Immediately upon arrival, we learned that our belongings would be going into storage because our house was already filled with Big Mama's things. I didn't think it was too much of a problem because we were going to be renovating the house as soon as possible. Then Big Mama made it known that none of her stuff or her friend's stuff would be moved out until their house was finished. This was not in the plan, but the kids and I tried to have a routine as much as we could: work, school, and church to keep down any confusion about what Big Mama was doing right in front of them. Unfortunately, that didn't stop them from asking, "Is Big Mama sleeping with that man?" If she wasn't embarrassed, I most certainly was for her.

Not liking the way things were going at the house, Scott decided to talk to his commanding officer about a transfer to Kings Bay Naval Station in St. Mary's, Georgia. With this arrangement, he would have to commute three hours every day, but at this point it was a lot better than being eight hours away. Scott really wanted to be close to the family and believed the Lord would move for him. He prayed for it to happen, often quoting Romans 4:17, and with faith his request was approved by the beginning of 2009. We thought things would start to turn around for us, especially with Scott being home, but I could never have imagined the turn of events that would take place in the span of one week. Scott, the kids, and I had started attending church regularly, and one sermon that Pastor was preaching really caught our attention: "Getting your house in order." It was something we had never really thought about until that very moment. What kind of example were we setting for our kids with Big Mama and her friend sleeping together in the next room? We left church that day knowing we had to say something to address the situation in a respectful way.

Knowing that whatever we said would offend them, Scott and I decided not to address her shacking up, but instead asked her when their house would be ready. She never answered our question; her response was "I'll be out by the end of next week." Big Mama didn't speak with us the rest of the time she was in the house with us. It wasn't until later that we found out from the family that she told everyone we had put them out.

Shortly after Big Mama moved all her stuff out, we began moving our things into the family home. There was a lot of cosmetic work to be done, and we knew it would cost more than what we had in our savings. Scott and the boys did most of the renovations. It came to a point where everything in our savings was gone, so we charged up two Home Depot cards. It was hard to comprehend that we had accomplished so much work, but there was still a lot to be done. The only thing we could think to do was to take out a loan to finish all the work, and with Scott and I both working, we could afford to refinance. We talked with a loan officer about our plans, and though they told us everything looked good on paper, they could not say what we could borrow on the house until they sent someone to do an appraisal.

We were so excited on the day of the appraisal because of all the work we had accomplished on our home. It was a blessing, and we just knew God would move for us. We had examined our home and gotten everything in order, started going to church, and even tithed whenever we could. We were finally ready for some much-needed relief. Even though things had not been what we expected at first, we just knew everything was going to turn around for us—that is, until the appraiser set foot on the property. Despite all the work, he didn't seem impressed in the slightest. He just kept saying, "I can't say as of yet, but I'll let your lenders know the market value of your home's worth when I return to my office." As the appraiser began to leave, I couldn't help but think what would happen if we didn't get the loan. What were we going to do? Well, the only thing we could do was wait.

It was about a week later, and we still hadn't heard anything from the lender. At this point, we were tired of waiting and decided to give them a call ourselves to find out the status of our loan. "It's approved…It has to be," I said to myself as we waited for him to say those magical words. "Please, let it be approved," I pleaded silently. "Oh, Mr. Styles about your loan," he stated as I cringed in anticipation. "At this time, we cannot approve your loan. Unfortunately, the comparable properties in your area are worth less than what you want to borrow."

In an instant, everything shattered. How could this possibly be? We had done so much work to this house, and now the only thing we had to show for it was more bills and an increasing house payment! We had planned everything out, and it had all fallen through. We simply didn't know what to do next, so we did what we could and prepared for Scott's retirement in 2010. We figured we would save some money with him not having to make the hour-and-a-half commute to work every day.

Thankfully, Scott found a job working as an engineer two months before his retirement date. "With his income and his retirement income, we should be fine," I told myself to get through. "Plus, I got a promotion at my job… we will manage." Among all the thoughts swarming in my head, I began to think on previous Bible study lessons and past sermons at church. I couldn't help but wonder if we were actually applying the teachings to our lives or just letting them go in one ear and out the other. The more I began to think, the more I began to realize that we hadn't even asked God about any of these things before we sought after them, yet we had expected Him to bless them. We hadn't been giving our full tithe, and we were sowing on infertile ground. I came to the sad reality that we were a spiritual mess. How could we possibly expect the Lord's full blessings?

Even after this revelation, we still tried our best to work it out ourselves, paying for appraisal after appraisal only to be met with the same answer, "NO!" We were so used to everything going our way and having whatever we wanted. We couldn't understand why it wasn't working out for us, but deep down, I knew. I knew it was time for a change, time to start doing things differently. I discovered that we had tied all our hopes, dreams, and feelings to people and other worldly things.

"For where your treasure is there will your heart be also" (Matthew 6:21). I figured it was now time to convince my husband what the Lord had laid on my heart about tithing. It was time to really grab hold of and try what our leaders had been teaching us at church. I knew it would be a lot for Scott to understand where I was coming from, especially with everything being as tight as it was with our money now. We knew that if we tithed like we were supposed to, it would be like having two mortgages, but at this point what did we have to lose? We decided for the first time that we would completely follow what the word says. I wish I could say that after tithing things immediately got better. It was easy to pay tithes because we had committed ourselves to giving God our first of everything; however, all of the issues we created didn't just go away. They were still our issues to deal with. As time went on, I ended up losing my job due to unforeseen circumstances. As a result, we couldn't afford the payments on the house and had to foreclose and file for bankruptcy by the end of 2011. We left our home, leaving the keys behind on the counter.

Despite everything, from 2012 to 2017, we were able to give our tithes, pay the rent on our apartment, save money, and pay all our bills, including bankruptcy, with no problem. Oddly enough, we didn't skip a beat. We had more than we'd ever had just doing what was right. The Lord even worked everything out with the lender selling the house, and we didn't have to pay anything back. We were seeing the blessings of the Lord manifest in our lives in our down season (Malachi 3:10).

By May of 2017, we had paid our bankruptcy off early and both of our credit scores had soared into the 700s. In June of the same year, we were investigating what we needed to prepare ourselves to buy a home in the next two years, because by the normal bankruptcy rules, "No one would dare give you a loan for at least two years." We called around, gave our information, and explained our circumstances, completely prepared to hear what we needed to do to get things started. We knew what people said, but we also knew what God said. It has now been six months since we moved into our newly built home in January 2018, and we are still seeing the blessings of God manifest in our lives. "As for God, his way is perfect..." (2 Samuel 22:31).

As for Big Mama, our relationship has improved over the last couple of years. I learned to love past any misunderstandings or hurt. I want to enjoy her as she grows older, cherishing every birthday, Mother's Day, and Christmas. I know tomorrow is not promised to anyone, and I refuse to live with regret (James 4:14).

ABOUT

Lady Walikqua M. Johnson

Lady Walikqua M. Johnson is a native of the Bronx but currently lives in South Carolina. Prior to relocating she was an NYPD Explorer and an active member of Higher Praise Community Church. It was during this time that she realized she was called to preach the gospel and was made a youth minister. Lady Walikqua later left that ministry and became an active member of Road to Damascus Ministry of God, Inc. There, she served under the leadership of Pastor Eugene Johnson and Co-Pastor Doris Johnson.

Currently, Lady Johnson is enrolled at ECPI University, where she will receive her Bachelor of Science degree in healthcare administration in January 2019. Lady Walikqua serves with her husband, Bishop Anthony P. Johnson I, of Unity Cathedral Church & Greater Vision Church. She is completely devoted to her husband and their four children Royal, Prince, Phillip, and Dymond.

Email:	walikquajohnson15@gmail.com
Phone:	929 431 0014
Facebook:	WalikquaJohnson

THE BISHOP'S WIFE

By Lady Walikqua M. Johnson

The Beginning

Where do I begin?! I was nineteen years old when I met my husband. No. I was actually eighteen going on nineteen. Keep in mind that my husband is twenty years my senior. He's dark chocolate with kissable lips, gorgeous eyes, and a hint of gray on his naturally curly hair. He also has a smile that'll make your heart melt. This is what initially attracted me to him, along with the intoxicating smell of Tiamo men's cologne. Okay, let me get out of feelings and continue with what I was originally trying to say before I got distracted by my husband. As you can tell, he still lights my fire today.

I met Bishop Johnson, AKA my husband, on the social media platform Myspace. This was when Myspace was the thing! If you knew anything about the platform, you're probably thinking…what? Yes. Myspace, honey! At that time, Myspace was the place to go before Facebook. It was a site where you had your own personal page, and we were able to design it, customize it, and apply music. When someone clicked on your page, your playlist would come on and they could jam to your style of music while scrolling through your information.

I remember logging on and receiving a message from him. I immediately thought to myself, *here I go again*. I say this because I was just getting out of a relationship and I didn't want to be bothered with people, especially "church people." I was going through some personal issues, and the last thing on my mind was getting involved with someone before being healed from my previous relationship. But one day, I decided to respond to his message. I gave him a call because he mentioned in his message that he was opening up a church and said that I should give him a call if I was interested.

We talked briefly that night, and really, from that night on, it was all she wrote. We've been together ever since.

Playing Church

Fast forward a few years and we were married with two baby boys named Prince and Royal. Now I was the wife of the bishop. I was a young wife, too. We married when I was twenty-five years old. Honestly, at that point it hadn't really hit me that I was a wife to a pastor. All I knew was I was married to the man I loved and our family was growing. I never took into consideration that I would eventually have to share him with others.

When he started his ministry in South Carolina, I wasn't too enthused about it. I really didn't want to be in church. I didn't want to have all those responsibilities. Plus, I was always annoyed with people because it seemed like they always had his time and I seemed to be competing with them for it. This made me distant. I thought that all I had do was be pretty and be the wife and everything would be okay. But that didn't work. Therefore, I found myself playing church because this was what I knew how to do. I would clean up well. I would dance, shout, and do all the "church" stuff, and I thought I'd get through it. But I quickly discovered that ministry was so much more than that. But I still kept thinking, *I'm the wife now. Why should he have to do this for people? Why should they always get his attention? Why does he has to answer every call?* Every time I turned around, all I heard was "Pastor this, Pastor that." And all I could think was, *Why are these people so needy?* I had so many questions. And I was so unhappy.

But by the time we had our second child, I began to like people a little bit more. I began to understand them a little better. Even though I still wasn't in a place where I was completely comfortable with being first lady and having people in my husband's face all the time, I was adjusting. We were living on Patterson Avenue in Roanoke, Virginia, and even though I was adjusting and smiling and telling the members I love you, underneath I was sinking. I was losing my own internal battle. I was so sad and felt so alone. I had a bad case of postpartum depression, and not many people knew this, not even my family. But it was so bad that I cut all my hair off because I wanted to feel different. I wanted to look different. I no longer wanted to be Lady Johnson. I didn't want a divorce, but by this time I felt like the real me was gone. After trying to be the person everybody else wanted me to be, I finally broke.

From Playing Church to Not Going at All

At one point I stopped going to service because I just couldn't stand to hear church stuff. Praise and worship sounded terrible, even if there were great singers singing. I just wasn't into it anymore. When I would hear the word being preached, I found myself drowning them out and wandering off thinking about something else. My body would be in service, but my mind was far away. I even thought that if I went to a "white" Baptist church, maybe things would have changed. But I was even more bored and annoyed. Not that there's anything wrong with going there, it just wasn't what I was used to. I was raised Baptist, but I'm Pentecostal to the bone.

I went from playing church to not going at all. I was unhappy, so it was easy for me to backslide and run to the world. My mindset was that I would stop for a while and do whatever I wanted. Since I come from a long line of drinkers, I fell into that trap, too. In the church world, they call it a generational curse. Looking back now, I can honestly say I was being selfish and I was unstable. I found myself playing with God and God's people. When things were great at home, I did what I was supposed to do in ministry and church. But when things were bad or weren't what I wanted, I would put God on the back burner. Then, I finally decided I was done. Thinking back, it's amazing how we "the saints" treat God. We call on Him when we need Him, and once HE blesses us or give us what we THINK we want, we forget about Him. We want to stop attending church services, we want to stop listening to our leaders. The Bible clearly states: **Jeremiah 3:15** *And I will give you pastors according to mine heart, which shall feed you with knowledge and understanding.* Also **Hebrews 13:17** *Obey them that have the rule over you, and submit yourselves: for they watch for your souls, as they that must give account, that they may do it with joy, and not with grief: for that is unprofitable for you.* King James Version (KJV).

I was mixed up and confused being in my flesh. I was reminded of these scriptures, and it scared me. I began to think and question the Lord. I would ask, "Lord, what is happening to me? Why do I not want to be in service anymore? Why do I feel so stuck?" People who knew us thought we had the best marriage, but on the inside we were torn to pieces. I had lots of questions for God: "Am I strong enough? Am I worthy enough? How did I get here?" I remember telling my husband, "I'm sorry, but I cannot do this anymore and I don't want to be in trouble with God." I felt like I was hindering him from his assignment. Yes. I wanted to do ministry alongside him, but my heart wasn't fully there. I didn't have the heart of a pastor. My thoughts were that God had assigned him, not me.

I've learned that so many people, especially some desperate woman, think that being the first lady is glamorous. Many think our job is simple. In reality, it's a shame how badly first ladies get dogged out, mistreated, and stepped on because WE'RE NOT the pastor. We have to wear many hats. It becomes overwhelming and we want to throw in the towel and quit because we're human, too. We get to see firsthand what our spouses go through and how people mistreat them. This was a major issue for me and part of the reason I couldn't stay stable. I'd often ask my husband, "How could you allow people to treat you any kind of way and still treat them with love and respect?" His answer was simple: "I deal with people right where they are. If they're a liar, you know they're a liar. If they're a thief, you know they're a thief and you treat them accordingly. You don't have to be nasty or mean. You'll know how to deal with them." And then it made sense! I have a very wise husband.

Hearing God's Voice Changes Things

I forgot what exactly I was doing or where I was, but I heard God's voice as clear as day. I was in one of my moods where I didn't want to be bothered with "church people." In my head, they were all cutthroat and meant us no good. Even the ones you think have your back…THEY DON'T! I heard God say, "You're going to be thirty years old soon. When are you going to take your salvation seriously?" Honestly, I thought at this point that I had really lost it. For sure, I thought I was going crazy. I thought that I must have been going out of my mind to hear a voice when no one was there. I heard it for a second time, and if I can describe it, it was like a calmness came over me. As I heard God, my world came together and it was peaceful. HIS voice was peaceful. My heart began to smile, my spirit was lifted, and my mind shifted. All in that very moment.

The Lord said, "Get on your phone and find somebody preaching my word." I did just that. I took out my iPhone and went to YouTube and searched for Juanita Bynum. I love me some her, but that wasn't who God directed me to this time. And it made sense because I understood what God said that time. I went to the search button on the top right corner, and I kid you not. The Lord dropped Dorinda Clark-Cole in my spirit and said, "Her." And it was an amazing feeling. But how was I going to translate what had happened to my husband when hours before I hadn't wanted anything to do with him, his church, or the people he shepherded? I kept thinking how I was going to tell him and how he would receive it.

Usually, if something's on my heart it burns me. I really have to get it out. But this time, every time I wanted to share with my husband, I couldn't say much. It was like God was holding my tongue. So I started listening to Mrs. Cole preaching sermons and songs. Even though I knew of her and I knew about two of her songs, I really had no idea who this amazing woman was in the Lord. I started to listen to her using my Bluetooth headphones and it became a part of my daily routine. No matter if I was at home or at work or even driving, anytime I had free time, I was listening to Dorinda Clark. Old sermons, new sermons, old songs, new songs, live shows. It didn't matter because I was so hungry and thirsty for the word. After a few long weeks of being disobedient, I felt so far behind that I needed to catch up. I needed to take my salvation seriously. I needed to be one with my husband, but God had to do it, not me.

One night we were in service and the service was high, meaning the spirit of the Lord was in the house. The prophetic words were going forth, and all I can remember is I went in. I went in so hard that at the end of the night my husband had seen the difference in me without me even saying one word. When we got home to West Main Street in Salem, Virginia, we talked about how service was so good and how all the prophetic words were on point. Prince intervened and said, "Mommy was crying and talking in tongues." My husband said, "Yeah you went in. You were walking and touching the chairs, speaking to the chairs and praying over the kids." He said that he said to himself, "She's serious!" At that moment, I was able to open my mouth and tell him what the Lord had done. I told him how serious it was for me this time. That no matter what happens, I'm taking my salvation seriously. The scripture says: **Philippians 2:12** *Work out your own salvation with fear and trembling.* King James Version (KJV).

Putting My Life Back Together

Since I had to go through the process of what looked like a never-ending thing, I can happily say I made it through. When it didn't look like God was listening to me or answering my prayers, HE was! He had to prepare me for my assignment, even though I kept running from it. Although I'm still finding my way, the way is clearer now. My thought process is different. My wants and priorities when it comes to ministry are in order now. It will never be easy, but I now know how to handle things a lot better than I did. I no longer allow things to get to me so easily. I can proudly say that through all of this, my prayer life has changed. I can proudly say I love people and I'm not pretending. I am strong. I am healed. I understand everything a little bit better. I wear the hat and fill the shoes of a bishop's wife with confidence and elegance. I stand in the gap for any young or mature woman who may be in my shoes and doesn't know which way to turn or doesn't know who to trust or talk to because this is a lonely road. Here's a piece of my testimony. I'm just like you!

ABOUT
Deneen Cooper

Deneen Cooper is the president of Uplift and Impact Career Counseling LLC, founded in 2011 to "uplift and impact the lives of individuals by acknowledging strengths and limiting weaknesses." Being in the field of human resources for twenty-six years and working for some of the largest organizations in the world enabled her to know the reasons companies make the hiring decisions they do. She realized it was her divine mission and gift to counsel people with valuable career information after surviving breast cancer and becoming disabled with spinal disease. Living with serious health challenges gives a perspective of GOD'S calling on you. Life is too short to waste your GOD-Given gifts and not live in your purpose.

"The heart of a man plans his way but the Lord establishes his steps" Proverbs 16:9

She is now embarking on a long-time desire to be an author. Deneen is single and has resided in the Bronx for fifty-three years. She is a daughter to her eighty-four-year-old father, a sister to her two brothers, and a University of North Carolina alum who bleeds Carolina blue and white. GO TARHEELS!!!

Phone:	917-747-1994
Email:	deneenblessed@aol.com dcblessed@outlook.com
Facebook:	Deneen Cooper
Twitter:	@upliftimpact
Instagram:	deneenblessed
LinkedIn:	deneenuplift

MY FAITH IS BIGGER THAN MY FEAR HOW I SURVIVED BREAST CANCER THREE TIMES

By Deneen Cooper

There are three words that no one wants to hear, and now I heard them for the second time. Deneen, the biopsy results came back, the cells tested were malignant, and "you have cancer." I said, "I have cancer again." On April 19, 2018, my world was turned upside down. As I sat in a hotel room in Rocky Mount, North Carolina, with my brother Kenneth, I kept saying that this couldn't be happening. I was preparing to be the emcee for a program we were doing for my dad that evening. I was in shock. The wave of tears came one after another. Kenneth hadn't heard me cry like this since the day after Mommy had passed away fourteen years before. I was inconsolable. Five years ago, it seemed like a dream—a dream that I woke up from when I had the lumpectomy procedure and seven weeks of radiation. It was supposed to be over. I prayed and thought I heard GOD say it was over. I had not foreseen that this disease would rear its ugly head in my life again. Now I was about to embark on another journey with this disease that would take me through crazy highs and lows. It would test me in ways that I could not prepare for, but even through all the uncertainty, I just knew deep inside I would be okay.

As I arrived back home ready to face the inevitable, I knew I needed some warriors. I called my cousin Cheryl, who is a physician, and told her I needed to explore all my options. In the back of my mind, I had pretty much decided what I was going to do. I just needed someone to be in agreement. I couldn't discuss this with my dad or my brothers. I thought about baring my soul to my niece but she had lost her mom to this dreaded disease at just thirty-seven years of age. I just couldn't burden her with the weight of my diagnosis.

Dr. Cheryl Clark is my awesome cousin who doesn't like any of her family to use her title. She lets us know in no uncertain terms, "I am your cousin first, a physician second." Having a family member who understands things from a clinical perspective is such a blessing. She has always been my second opinion, and I thank GOD for the rock she has been through all of this. When we talked, I had already made the decision to have a mastectomy. I just knew in my spirit that this would be my only option. No truer words had ever been spoken.

The decision to have parts of your body removed is traumatic. I guess I didn't really think about it with the lumpectomy because only a part with the malignant cells is removed. The misshapen breast that was left after that procedure should have been the realization, but it is truly different than full removal. As much as I wanted to think about it, I had something else to focus on. I was heading to a women's retreat in Myrtle Beach, South Carolina, right before Mother's Day. GOD had laid on my spirit that I needed to be more active and get back to what I loved to do—travel! My limited movement from spinal disease had caused me to be cautious about traveling, and now I was pushing past that fear. It was one of the best decisions, as it was life changing. I met women from all over the country, and we will be connected forever because of the move of GOD at this retreat. I had healing hands placed on me. The woman of GOD who hosted the retreat has the gift of prophecy. She prophesized that I was facing this disease because the attack of Satan saw what GOD had in store for me: to be able to share my story as an author. This was confirmation, as I had just become an author last year. What did this all mean? Whatever GOD was trying to tell me, I was definitely listening.

As I returned home, basking in the glow of this retreat, reality hit me right in the face. With medical appointments with my oncology and plastic surgeons and a surgery date in early June, I didn't have a lot of time to let fear set in. In retrospect, fear was right at the surface of my thoughts, but I had to focus. I was about to have major surgery, but this time I really felt as if my life hung in the balance. My oncology surgeon had shared that a mastectomy really had been my only option. We had decided on a mastectomy of the left breast with abdominal flap reconstruction. In layman's terms, tissue would be removed from my abdomen to reconstruct the left breast after removal of the malignant cells and breast tissue. The highlight of the surgery was the free tummy tuck that would occur. Everything was going forward as planned, but my spirit was uneasy. I kept thinking to myself that I should just have both breasts removed.

If they were able to perform all these procedures in one surgery, I told my oncology surgeon, let's just take them both. He gave me pushback, as there had never been any issues with my right breast. I told him it would give me peace of mind as I came into this world with these breasts and they should be removed together. This decision would be one that would impact my life forever.

On June 4, 2018 at Beth Israel Medical Center, I underwent a bilateral mastectomy with abdominal flap reconstruction to remove this disease from my body. It was a ten-hour surgery, and I was hospitalized for four days. Every aspect of my initial post-surgery healing that was shared by my physicians and a Sista friend who had undergone the procedure rang true. It was no joke, but not from a pain perspective. Let me paint the visual. When I left the hospital, I had four surgical drains releasing blood and fluids from my body. I had to sleep in a recliner for four weeks because I couldn't lie on the remaining drain that was finally removed on July 5. My best friend, Vee, was here for the first five days after my surgery, along with homecare nurses. Thank GOD for these women warriors and Sista friends who came to the hospital and my home days after the surgery. GOD even made it possible for my family who was here from Florida to come by and see me as well. All this love was a major part of the healing process, and I surely needed it. I also thank GOD for my younger brother, Kenneth, the same brother who was with me when I received my diagnosis. I don't call it coincidence because coincidence is GOD'S way of remaining anonymous.

Let me tell you what I've learned about illness. People make you either a priority or an option. I am a witness—not to listen to what people say, but to watch what they do. I have become wary of those who tell me they understand what I am going through. Unless you are inside my body and can feel what I feel, then no, you don't. We all know those family members and friends who believe they are medical professionals and want to tell you what to do with your body. This is why I believe so many who suffer with this disease don't discuss their diagnosis. Instead of telling someone you understand and what they should do, all they really need is for you is to just listen and be present.

My relationship with GOD is all that I have at times, and that relationship is all that I will ever need. I am unapologetic about GOD healing me. I spoke the truth that GOD healed me when I was first diagnosed in 2012, and I speak that truth now. My transparency through this health journey is because GOD told me to share it with anyone who will listen. There is no test without a testimony, and GOD said, "Yours will bless so many people." What I've learned about healing is that most of it is mental and spiritual. The majority of my body was reconstructed—or maybe "restored" is a better word. The physical part will heal in due time, but the mental part needs the spiritual part to truly become whole. Speaking my healing into existence—this is still a work in progress for me, but just when I thought this chapter in my story was written, GOD said, "NOT YET."

Unexplainable things happen in this lifetime. That is where your faith in a power higher than yourself becomes real. Remember how I had received pushback from my oncology surgeon not to perform a bilateral mastectomy? The surgery would be ten hours long, and there had never been any problems with my right breast. As much as I highly respected my surgeon's opinion because he had removed cancer from my breast the first time, there was a feeling in my spirit that I had made the best decision for me. Three weeks after my surgery, I received a call from my oncology surgeon to discuss the pathology report. "Deneen, praise GOD for that voice you heard. Based on the results of this report, cancer cells were found in your right breast, the breast that had never shown any signs of malignant cells, even through numerous mammograms and ultrasounds over a six-year period. With all the surgery you just had to remove this disease, it would have still have been in your body." As I let his statement penetrate to the core of my being, all I could utter was, "BUT GOD." I could not allow myself to sit in that truth because I know GOD still performs miracles. I am a walking, breathing testimony of GOD doing things in divine order. People wonder why I am so vocal about my journey. Until I take my last breath, I will share who, what, when, where, and how GOD healed me!

I know for sure that GOD has always had a purpose for my pain. Through it all, no weapon formed against me will ever prosper. I am a living example of GOD'S healing in action. Don't get me wrong—this journey is not for the faint of heart, and many days will not be easy. So many who have been diagnosed have not survived, and I honor and cherish their memories. I always believed I would live, and because I know GOD saved me, I will always share my story. I survived breast cancer three times because my FAITH IS BIGGER THAN MY FEAR!!!

ABOUT

Dr. LaWana Richmond

Dr. LaWana Richmond is passionate about Afrofuturism for many reasons—including her enjoyment of all forms of media in the genre—but more recently because of its value as a framework for connecting underrepresented students to STrEAM fields and underserved communities to economic and social planning and development. She recently co-organized the Afrofuturism Lounge, an after-party/counter-con event for Black comic creators, writers, artists, animators, and publishers to share their stories and wares with a diverse audience. Dr. Richmond works at the University of California, San Diego, where she manages organizational development and process improvement for transportation services and lectures on higher education administration and governance in addition to Afrofuturism.

Website:	www.firyali.com
	www.afrofuturismlounge.com
Facebook:	firyvisions
Instagram:	@firyvisions
Twitter:	@firyvisions

LOSING MY WAY WHILE FINDING MY PURPOSE

By Dr. LaWana Richmond

Throughout my adolescence and early adult years, I was a single parent with first one, and then two children while navigating my own maturation process. I was beginning the process of raising other people while also trying to raise myself. I loved each of my children without condition from the moment I learned of their presence within my womb. I must lead with this because my actions may not have nor may not in the future always seem to indicate that.

My earliest memory is of waking up on my knees in my bed with my right hand up near my ear with fading recollection of working with the elves on the North Pole to help them make toys for all the children of the world. I was about four years old. So, yes, service is part of my DNA. Part of getting to know myself as I came of age was reconnecting with this part of myself. At my very core, service to my community or fellow (wo)man is hardwired into my thought process.

When I first started at the university where I have worked for the past thirteen years, it was supposed to be a quick stop while I finished my master's degree in information systems. Within a few months, I realized I wanted to stick around for a bit. I appreciated the idea of work-life balance and having a mission beyond reaping dividends for stockholders. I also recognized the potential for personal and professional growth.

Within my first year, I asked one of my coworkers who had been at the U for a while what I would need to do in order to teach at the university. I'll never forget her response. She said, "Staff never becomes faculty." She may as well have waved a red flag in front of my face. At that moment, a part of me knew I would be the exception. I didn't know how, but I knew it was going to happen. That was in 2006.

From the very beginning, I made it a point to participate in the campus community and learn as much as I could about the way things work at a university. I volunteered, served on committees, and engaged in workshops, seminars, and conferences. I became so obsessed with making myself better that I forgot to acknowledge the accomplishments and progress already made. I was focused on the future.

Somewhere in all that focus, I lost sight of my son. When he was small, we were close. I took him with me pretty much every place I went. When he was a baby, I'd take him and his bouncer and have him at my feet during meetings and events. I carried him in a sling close to my chest so he could hear my heartbeat. I never imagined my baby boy would choose to go his own way.

My first clue was when he told me he didn't want to be successful. He wanted to just be regular. I realize now that one of my failings was not getting him to see that success is regular.

Before his teens, my son started to drift. He began to reject the values and guidelines that framed his early years. He was drawn to people and things that didn't align with my worldview. I never stopped loving my son, but it became harder for us to understand one another. Looking back, I know I could have listened more.

When my son was almost eighteen, we had a conflict that escalated to an ultimatum. He had to choose between following my rules or not living with me. He chose to not follow the rules. For all intents and purposes, that was the last time my son lived with me. Since then, he has spent a few days or weeks with me when he has hit a snag, but for the most part, he has been on his own.

Since his departure from my home, we have often not seen eye to eye. I looked at him and his life through the lens of a mother, and all I saw was wasted potential. I saw a young man who was selling himself short because he was treating life like a game of checkers instead of chess. As his mother, I wanted him to stop and think. I wanted him to realize how much he has to offer. I wanted him to see how amazing he is.

I believe he heard my words as criticisms. I believe he thought my praise was biased because I'm his mother. I believe he thought my love for him blinded me to his flaws. I don't know what was going on in his head, but his words and actions pushed me away. I'm sure my words and actions were having the same effect on him. We were harsh with one another.

I never gave up on my son. I love(d) him too much for that. I did, however, practice tough love. It was hard not to just give him everything he asked for. It was hard to let him find his own answers (particularly in this climate). My son has been 6' 4" tall since his mid-teens. Every time I turned on the TV, I saw another young man who looked like him and had been the victim of police brutality or vigilante "justice." When President Obama said if he had a son, he'd probably look like Trayvon, I totally related because I have a son. My son looks more like Mike Brown, though. Every time my son walked away angry or hung up on me, I felt a chill go down my spine. I was always afraid of something happening to him.

In the fall of 2012, I had minor surgery and was sent home heavily sedated. I let my son borrow my car because I knew I wasn't going anywhere anytime soon. I was that out of it. Later that evening, the phone rang. Even though I still wasn't feeling well, I answered because it was my son. His first words were, "The police hit me." I was instantly awake. I was terrified. It turns out, the police had hit my car. I had my partner take me to where my son was because regardless of who was at fault, I didn't want my son alone at night on a dark street with some strange police officer. It worked out. Everyone was okay. The police officer had put his foot on the accelerator instead of the brake and rear-ended my vehicle. Fortunately, he had a citizen riding along with him, so there was a witness. This was just one of many times I was particularly afraid of what was going to happen with my son.

Letting go and letting God was not an easy choice, but it seemed like the best choice when it came to my son. He had his mind made up about most things and allowed me little or no influence. Rather than fight all the time and fight losing battles, I let him find his way and held on to my faith that he would remember who he is. My son had always been very bright and wise beyond his years. He just wanted to live life on his own terms. Those terms were often not consistent with the values and principles upon which I had built his foundation.

It was scary, and I was often worried that I couldn't just call him up to see how he was doing or go check on him somewhere. I usually didn't know where he was staying, and when he had a phone, he didn't always answer when I called. When he did answer, the conversations were usually brief and superficial at best and confrontational at worst. Sometimes, I felt like I only really heard from him when he needed something. I was the B of M (Bank of Mom). Looking back, that was actually a good thing. At least somewhere beneath all the resentment, he knew he could come to me if he really needed me and I would do what I could to help. All the same, those interactions usually culminated in angry words and hurt feelings.

Now, my son has a son, and suddenly, it all makes sense to him. Now that he has someone of his own to love and care for, it seems like things have finally started coming full circle. He and I have begun the process of dialog—not only about the future but about things that happened in the past. I believe he has opened his heart to me and is more receptive to guidance. At the same time, I believe I am learning to see him as a grown man. At 26, he is mature beyond his years and has seen and experienced things of which I have no knowledge. My son has raised himself into a man I am learning to appreciate and respect.

When we talk these days, if it's not about his son, it's about the life he's had, the life he's built, or the life he's building. I appreciate knowing the seeds of values I tried so hard to instill in him when he was young are finally bearing fruit. I realize that we may have a falling -out tomorrow (I'm just saying), but I am overjoyed by the knowledge that we can get back to this place.

Incidentally, I received my first faculty appointment this summer at the university where I work. It took twelve years from when I first became curious, but it happened. Never say never. I am still very much engaged in community service. It is currently my work in Afrofuturism that allows me to combine my interest in community development with my interests in science, technology, engineering, science fiction, and other abstract arts, but I allow it to express in the micro and macro levels based on how, when, and where the Spirit moves me.

Patience, love, and listening have been our friends. My grandmother used to have a pillow that said, "If you love someone, let them go. If they come back to you, they're yours forever, and if they don't, they never were." I thought it only applied to romantic relationships, but I see this at work with my son and my daughter. With each of them, I had to let go. I had to let them go their way and find their way back to me. A big part of the evolution of my relationships with each of my children was getting to a place where I acknowledge their maturity and appreciate them as adults. When I spoke to them as the man and woman they are, they responded with respect and appreciation for the mother and woman I am and have always been. We each had to acknowledge our own imperfections and love each other's whole selves.

ABOUT

Toni Coleman Brown

Toni Coleman Brown is an author, coach, marketing expert, and motivational speaker. She is also the CEO and founder of the Network for Women in Business, an online community for women business owners who seek affordable cutting-edge training and the ability to connect and advance with other like-minded individuals. The motto for the Network is "We EDUCATE to ELEVATE women in business." Toni is also the host and creator of the Small Business Bootcamp for Women and the Online Marketing Mastermind Live events.

Toni has been featured in the *New York Amsterdam News*, the *Network Journal Magazine*, *Our Time Newspaper*, Black Enterprise Online, *Working Woman Magazine*, and WPIX 11's Working Woman Report. She is the author of Quantum Leap: How to Make a *Quantum Leap in Your Network Marketing Business* and the compiler and co-author of *Network to Increase Your Net Worth* and *Delayed But Not Denied: 20 Inspirational Stories of Life and Resiliency.*

Toni is on a mission to fulfill her God-ordained purpose of changing the lives of millions. Toni lives in Queens, New York, with her husband and two daughters.

Toni can be reached at:
Email: toni@networkforwomeninbusiness.com
Website: www.tonicolemanbrown.com
Facebook: tonicolemanbrown
Twitter: @tonibrown
Instagram: tonicolemanbrown
Pinterest: toni1266

MALWARE SCARE AND A PRAYER

By Toni Coleman Brown

When you're on vacation, you expect no headaches, no distractions, and no emergencies. But when I received a text message saying that my website was being re-directed elsewhere, I immediately looked at all the sites I owned, even those I managed for, my clients and every single one had been injected with malware. My first thought was, "OMG! This is going to cost me a lot of money to fix." But my second thought was, "Just chill."

I woke up the next at around five o'clock the next morning, and something told me to watch YouTube to see if I could fix the problem myself. I stumbled upon a video that showed me exactly what I could do to remove the malware, but the task was daunting. Yet I had to give it a try. It took me literally all day to finish. But I did it with a positive attitude. This was because I had attended church the night before and had heard my brother preach for the first time. His words were a right-now-and-on-time message. I felt as if he was ministering directly to me.

When I'd walked into church that evening, I was surprised to see him playing the organ and singing "This Little Light of Mine" during praise and worship. Then he began to deliver the word, which was all about success requiring sacrifice. His words moved me because they made me realize that with every level of success there is some level of pain. This incident of having my sites injected with malware was just one of those instances. His message gave me the perspective and the fortitude I needed to plow through the task at hand.

Removing the malware was an arduous process. I got so frustrated that I started to delete some of my websites that I didn't actively use. But I made some mistakes. I deleted two niche sites that were receiving a nice amount of traffic and were generating AdSense income for me. I kicked myself because I could have done something with those sites to make them better. But I never took the time to analyze them. Just like that, all the files were gone. And when I did look at the analytics, it was too late.

After I removed all the malware, the WordPress software application stopped functioning altogether. I'd broken it. I had to downgrade to a lower version and then uninstall and reinstall it, along with all my plugins. Then, like magic, everything started working again. I immediately began to secure all the sites and started to rethink my whole strategy.

After giving it some thought, I realized that this malware attack was the best thing that had ever happened to me. Releasing myself from the burden of having all those sites that I didn't use forced me to rethink my overall business strategy and do more investigating—both under the hood of my business and regarding my inner self. I learned a lot as a result.

I learned that I am an incredibly tech-savvy woman, and I am so thankful for that. I am also all over the place because of my interests, and I have a lot of them. I am interested in healthy living, personal finance, online marketing, publishing, and network marketing. But of all things, I am a trainer, facilitator, course creator, and life-changer. My ultimate goal has been to create an online university of sorts. Years ago, I purchased the URL www.mytrainingportals.com, which was supposed to be the catch all for my training courses. Little did I know back then that this URL would change everything for me.

Once I took the time to analyze my sites, I discovered that only two received any traffic at all and that the traffic wasn't so great. I knew that I could really scale down. Then I realized that only a few pages were garnering the most traffic, and one of those pages happened to be about continuous learning. It appears on the first Google search page for that term. I thought I was going to have to do a lot of work to get a clear strategy for the next ten years, but this mishap caused me to get it together fast. I realized that I could delete most of the pages on my websites. This provided an answer to a question that I had asked myself earlier this year: "What if I could only subtract to solve problems?" (I got this from Tim Ferris' *17 Questions That Changed My Life*).

Before this malware event, I had been working blindly in my business. I was basically existing without any long-term strategies or plans. I had a lot of short-term strategies, but none of them could take me to where I really wanted to go. I knew what I needed to do, but I was getting in my own way. Yet in my own clumsiness and naïveté, I did a lot of things right. The most important thing I did was not quit. Today, all roads lead to www. mytrainingportals.com. In all my areas of interest, I educate to elevate. Therefore, going forward, all paths in my funnel will lead to this amazing website where visitors will be able to discover their pathway (portal) to success. All of my online courses will be hosted there.

Portals are pathways. Pathways lead to discovery. At my core, I have always been the go-to person for guidance. Even my mother would tell me that. I am glad to finally have a place where I can pour out all my knowledge so that everyone can benefit from my gift.

I cannot put into words how happy I am. All I can say is that God is good. He will put you in situations that will make you uncomfortable—so uncomfortable that you will be forced to do something to turn it around. I realized that I had been sitting in my comfort zone for far too long. I had also been playing small for no reason at all. I had been giving advice to others but not taking it myself. This experience taught me that when I put what I know into action, I succeed. I know a lot. And I have helped a lot of people. I will never stop doing that. But in this season, I am going to help myself. I am going to invest and pour into me in a way that I've never done before. And I am going to continue to pray and serve God at my highest level, with the hopes that others will see Him in everything I do.

My malware attack was evil, but attending the church service and hearing my brother minister to the congregation was good. I am convinced that good always prevails over evil. I survived this test, and I will survive all the rest because I have been prepared for such a time as this. I am living my dream with full belief that the best is yet to come. Like the comedian Tiffany Hadish would say, "She READY!" Because guess what? She is!

ABOUT

Janelle Rollins-Johnson

Janelle Rollins-Johnson, founder of Vision Enterprise, is a writer, mentor, teacher, and strategist to those desiring to maximize their lives to achieve limitless potential.

She equips people to rise to the achievable challenge of their divine purpose and next level of greatness by teaching the principles of mind transformation. Janelle believes in everyone's ability to transcend adversity and overcome life's inevitable challenges. Whether individually or in a group environment, Janelle provides strategies to help ignite the fire that dwells within.

Vision Enterprise (visionenterprise360.com) is a human potential training company that teaches personal growth and development, life enrichment skills, and career and leadership skills.

Janelle is committed to helping unlock purpose and destiny for people to harness their potential and live the purpose-filled lives for which they were created.

Janelle resides in New York City. She is a wife and the mother of two amazing children.

Website: www.visionenterprise360.com

Phone: 917.636.5547

THREE STRIKES AND I'M STILL NOT OUT

By Janelle Rollins-Johnson

One morning as I was preparing to get to work looking for work, I was standing in front of the mirror and noticed that my face looked odd. Staring at my reflection, I saw that the left side was slightly sagging. When did this happen? I thought back to getting the kids up and ready for school. It had only been an hour since their dad had rushed them out the door to take them to school and then head to work. And both Keiths—father and son—surely would have noticed half of my face sagging when they kissed me goodbye. Jasmine would have been oblivious given her young age and morning grouchiness. That was after I had brushed my teeth and washed my face, which was before I even woke up the kids and prepared their breakfast. And my face wasn't sagging then, so this must have happened not too long ago. Instinctively, I called Keith. Following his instructions, I raised my arms and did the other tests used to detect a stroke or Bell's palsy as he instructed. It was neither. Thank God.

I didn't want to sit all day in the emergency room, so I monitored it closely throughout the day, looking in every mirror I passed—mainly the one in the main floor bathroom near the kitchen, the one in the foyer leading upstairs, and the ones in my bedroom and the adjoining bathroom. During one of my inspections while in the main floor bathroom, it appeared like my face was moving, like it was changing shape. The left side went from sagging to protruding in the cheek area in front of my left ear. Then the right side, which wasn't sagging, began to mirror the left side. Watching this happen to my reflection gave me the willies as memories of old horror films where creatures under the skin would pop out flooded my mind. I started poking my face just to make sure. It still had its usual softness, so I massaged it and tried to reposition it—like that was going to work. But I had to try something! By the evening, both sides of my face had protrusions in the areas in front of my ears that reminded me of Alvin, Simon, and Theodore. Having watched the *Alvin and the Chipmunks* movie multiple times with the kids, I had no doubt—I looked like a chipmunk!

When Keith and the kids got home that evening, we followed the usual routine, which began with high-pitched, fast-paced chatter as the kids filled me in on their day. When it was my turn to share, I realized that I was so preoccupied with my face and doing lots of online research to try to find answers that I hadn't done much else. I asked them if they noticed anything different about me. Their father did, which his eyes communicated, but it wasn't as apparent to the kids. I brought them to the living room and sat on the sofa, placing my three-year-old on my lap so she could more easily see my face. Again, I asked them if they noticed anything different about me. Jasmine looked me up and down, then shrugged and asked, "Like what?" Keith, four years older than his sister, positioned himself right in front of me and slowly inspected me. He said that he noticed something different but wasn't sure. So I touched both sides of my face in front of my ears and showed them how they were sticking out. I was surprised to feel how hard and stiff it had gotten. This gave me the willies all over again. My inquisitive son shot off a host of questions, none of which I could answer except for sharing how and when it happened. I asked them to pray for me and assured them that I would see a doctor if needed.

My prayers that night were all about my face, and the next morning when I looked in the bathroom mirror—still no change. I could feel that area of my face moving, but it didn't change shape. Boy, was that creepy. And I still looked like a chipmunk. I vacillated between going to the hospital and waiting another day to see my primary care physician. At the urging of my girlfriend, I went to the emergency room.

As with most emergency rooms, the neatly lined seats along the walls and in the center of the room were filled with people who were preoccupied with their own emergencies. By the looks of it, my noon arrival would have me there until that night, prevented me from getting home before Keith and the kids. To kill time, I called Keith and a few close friends to bring them up to speed, promising to fill them in after I spoke to the doctor. I was comforted to know they were all praying for me. But I had such discomfort watching the hands of the wall clock crawl forward as I impatiently sat there impulsively touching the hard protrusions that moved around at will. I shuddered, accelerating the mounting fear and rhetorical questions I asked myself. What is happening to me? Will I would look like this forever? Will my face change again into another, more gruesome distortion? Whatever this is, I pray there's a cure.

After the dreaded full day of waiting, I finally was seen by the doctor and explained my symptoms to him, sharing a selfie I had taken a week prior. His eyes widened and the pink in his skin vanished as he looked from the photo to me and then back to the photo. He slowly shook his head and stuttered, "I have never seen anything like this in my life!" He didn't mask his shock and disbelief as he prescribed antibiotics and told me to immediately see my PCP. I had spent all day in the ER just to get antibiotics?! Nevertheless, I took them while in the pharmacy, anxious for them to make my chipmunk cheeks disappear.

Sadly, the antibiotics produced no change, but I was able to get an appointment with my long time primary care physician within a few days. I was the first patient of the day, so I was ushered in immediately. When he saw my face and touched it, the creases intensified in his already creased forehead as he pressed his thin lips together and said, "Hmmm," conveying his grave concern. I was also overdue for my annual physical, so he had bloodwork done for both. After responding to his questions about the symptoms, I asked him a mountain of my own, but he didn't want to speculate without seeing the results from the bloodwork.

There was still no facial change three days later, and the results from my bloodwork were abnormal. He referred me to a series of specialists—four, to be exact. What followed was six months of all kinds of tests, needles, and specialists to accurately diagnose my condition. That spring, summer, and fall were filled with testing and prayers. Before the kids returned to school, we managed a trip to see my aging grandfather in Florida. I'm so glad we did because my life had been void of anything fun and I was extremely tired all the time. I didn't know if the fatigue was from all the running, the stress, the fervent praying, the illness, or all of the above. If I hadn't been included in the company-wide pre-buyout layoff that released over 1000 employees, I surely would have had to take a leave of absence. Look at God's timing.

I was grateful that I wasn't debilitated, and not having any pain was a blessing and kept my fear of having a terminal disease at bay. Aside from the facial distortion and extreme fatigue, the only other symptom was extreme weight loss. I had wanted to lose twenty pounds anyway, so I relished eating everything that pleased my palate that would normally appear on my waistline. I was indulging big time, ending almost every evening with my favorite—a pint of butter pecan ice cream. And when I would weigh myself, I would have the same look of shock and disbelief as the ER doctor when the numbers on the scale were lower. Since my high-fat, high-caloric diet seemed to accelerate my weight loss, I became a slim chipmunk. Or, shall I say, "Chipette." Go figure.

During my appt, my PCP had noticed swelling in my lacrimal glands. The area around the upper eyelid had always been "full" so I didn't notice that they were actually bigger. He referred me to an ophthalmologist—one of the four specialists.

My wait time at the ophthalmologist's office began with filling out the new patient forms. I took in my surroundings which were more intimate and inviting than other waiting rooms. The room had a slightly Asian decor with low black sofa-like seats, and two large pictures of Asian youth adorned the walls—one was a photo of a young girl with a blunt black bob cut to her earlobes and a single teardrop on her face. She had so much expression and innocence in her watery eyes. The other picture had several girls and boys, again with the eyes as the focal point. I guess it was apropos given the nature of their business. A small wall-mounted flat screen TV played one of the morning talk shows. And the glass table between both sofa-lined walls had a unique-looking glass bowl centerpiece with a few large magazines vertically lined up beside it. My comfortable surroundings made the hour wait more bearable. Despite my nine o'clock arrival, it appeared that some patients were being seen.

I was tired and disinterested in watching TV, so I closed my eyes and was left to my own thoughts. Please don't let this be hereditary. It's times like this that I wish I knew my family history. Aside from my mother losing her battle with breast cancer and my father's liver not sustaining his alcohol abuse, I know little about my family. My older sister, younger brother, and I grew up in foster care, which prevented me from having much knowledge about my relatives or if any of them experienced such symptoms for whatever condition

I had. Is this something my kids would get? And, if so, at what age? They would be terrified to feel and see their faces moving around and changing shape. Jasmine probably wouldn't realize any change. Her biggest concern would be like most toddlers—claiming everything as hers. But Keith would likely intellectualize his condition and announce his self-diagnosis with the authority of a specialist. Wearing size 5T slim pants that still fit loosely, his seven-year-old body couldn't take such drastic weight loss. As panic started rising I prayed, "Lord, please spare my children."

I had drifted off to sleep when I was called in to see the ophthalmologist. She did an in-depth exam, though I didn't understand what it had to do with the cheek protrusions. But, whereas my concern was my chipmunk cheeks, hers was my puffy upper eyelids. With a longer version of the hairstyle worn by the girl in the teardrop picture, she was polite, courteous, and professional with no social banter. The room was dimly lit with black shades that were drawn. This was not your regular eye exam room. Her tall, slim frame quickly scooted around the room on her wheeled chair as she worked with speed, precision, concentration, and focus. She took pictures of my eyes from every angle and then dilated them in preparation for another eye exam. I then had to go to two other more well-lit rooms for more testing with other staff. After a brief time in the waiting room, this time accompanied by two other waiting patients, I found myself back with the ophthalmologist to get my results. She suspected I had an uncommon condition that couldn't be cured, although it could be treated into remission. She said the inflammation of my lacrimal glands was part of it, and she prescribed 40mg of prednisone along with prednisone eyedrops and requested monthly follow-ups. She supported my PCP's suggestion to see a pulmonologist and wrote a note explaining what she suspected.

Two weeks later, during my initial pulmonology appointment, I went through intense and exhaustive breathing tests and had many vials of blood drawn. When the PAs were finished, the pulmonologist entered and I shared what I had been experiencing. He scheduled me for another type of exam where dye was injected to illuminate my internal organs. When I returned the following week for the results, he confirmed the ophthalmologist's diagnosis and explained that my case was caught early so it wasn't as severe as it could get. His expression was void of compassion as he emphasized the importance of taking my medication and being closely monitored. He adjusted the prednisone dosage and required me to come in for monthly testing. My face soon returned to its former shape, only to change again as I quickly gained weight from the prednisone. The doctor had warned me of that side effect, but it seemed to have happened overnight.

During my recovery, I noticed a bright red rash on the entire length and width of my outer right thigh. It was slightly raised from my skin but felt normal. Although it was painless, I couldn't stop staring at it in bewilderment. It appeared out of the blue—bright and red and massive. What in the world was this, and where had it come from? By the time I could get in to see my PCP, it had faded to the point that he couldn't diagnose it. He suspected it was related to the other condition and suggested I see the pulmonologist if it reappeared. Well, several days later, it did, this time on the inner part of my left leg extending around toward my calf. It was just as bright red, painless, elevated, massive, and irregularly shaped as the previous one. Fortunately, I could get in to see the pulmonologist the next day before it disappeared. He said it was not related to the condition and pulled some strings for me to get a biopsy immediately. Within days it disappeared again, but by the time another one appeared, the results from the biopsy had diagnosed it to be another uncommon disease. This one, appearing and disappearing at will, had no treatment or cure. Would it reappear on a more prominent and visible place like my face, chest, neck, or arms, causing me embarrassment or the need to have to explain it to people? Only a select few people knew about my health challenges, and unless it became life altering, I preferred to keep it that way. Thank God it eventually faded like the others and still hasn't reappeared.

Neither condition was serious or life threatening, but it made me wonder if the "rule of three" was real or just a coincidence that became a myth over time. The rash appeared three times. Although I was experiencing two conditions, was a third one on the horizon, making the rule of three real for me? It didn't take long to find out, as I was soon diagnosed with a third condition—one that was also deemed incurable.

There are specific times when my feet swell—while pregnant with Keith and Jasmine, and during hot summer days. It was fall, so neither was the case, and not only were my feet swollen but so were my legs. While my right foot and leg had significantly more inflammation than my left, I could no longer wear closed footwear other than loosely laced sneakers. My primary care physician referred me to a podiatrist.

As I sat in yet another waiting room, I was lost in thought as my positive attitude started to wane and I began to whine and complain. Why, God? Why am I experiencing so much hardship? I had a painful and lonely childhood—being teased and ostracized because of a third-degree burn on my left leg and foot; growing up in foster care without getting a chance to say "I love you" before disease claimed my mother and father; and being shifted from home to home and eventually separated from my siblings. Brokenness and unwise choices led to unhealthy relationships as a teen and young adult. Being deemed overqualified while having substantial financial responsibilities has caused a strain that's threatening to create marital discord. And now I'm dealing with consecutive health challenges. I don't want my children to experience growing up without their mother like I did. I want to shower them with the love, affection, nurturing, and guidance that I so desperately craved and needed growing up. Lord, please spare me to see my children grow up so I can guide and support them to become all that you created them to be!

Hearing my name called pulled me out of my pensive state, and with a heavy heart I followed the physician assistant. After the young podiatrist entered and greeted me, he asked questions and did some probing and testing before telling me his diagnosis—another persistent condition that has no cure. My heart grew heavy as I internally asked God, "What is going on here?"

** ** ** ** **

I had spent nearly two years dealing with health challenges one after the other, and during that ordeal, I was covered by God's grace and mercy. The diagnoses may have been uncommon and incurable, but they weren't common and terminal. They may have been unsightly, but they weren't debilitating and didn't cause significant pain. In my desire and quest for spiritual understanding, I believe God's purpose was to get my attention and to elevate my faith in Him. I easily professed my faith under the security of my paycheck with no health issues besides hypertension. So, I doubt the timing of my health challenges was happenstance. They began shortly after my layoff when I started obsessing over the bills. I started seeking what was familiar and convenient - positions in executive support and office management. I knew, however, that God was leading me to pursue career services and writing full-time, which I had been doing on the side for two decades. God was redirecting my career from the safe and familiar to the uncharted waters of divine destiny, though it came with lots of uncertainty. It required a level of faith that superseded convenience. Until I was confronted, I didn't realize that I trusted God in some areas more than others.

Like Jonah, my attempt to run—to stick with what was familiar—was met with being swallowed up in a situation that positioned me to stop running, submit, and trust God with every part of my life. He knew my health would get my attention. What good would a steady direct deposit do me if I'm not alive and well? My persistent health challenges sure put things into the proper perspective. Through it all, God was elevating me to an unprecedented level of faith in Him—over my health, career, and finances.

This experience taught me a lot about myself and my relationship with God. It was easy for me to trust God when life was going smoothly, but God wanted me to trust Him even when life didn't make sense. The lesson for me was in the process, not in the outcome.

I have yet to experience symptoms for the first two conditions. The doctors say they're in remission, but I believe I'm healed.

Once my health challenges no longer consumed me, I was able to focus on fully transitioning my career to writing, providing job readiness coaching and services and helping people elevate in their careers. Being able to help people become the best "vision" of themselves is extremely fulfilling, but it began with me—me trusting God.

As for my appearance—well, it took some time for me to switch from my decadent high-calorie diet, but once I did, I slowly shed most of the weight, and my energy level increased. I admit that miss my nightly butter pecan, but I do not miss those chipmunk cheeks. And although I'm still experiencing swelling in my legs and feet, thankfully, it's not debilitating or painful. Some days, I'm even able to wear my cute shoes.

---- ABOUT ----

Julia D. Shaw

Julia D. Shaw is a passionate entrepreneur with more than thirty years of professional experience. Julia's latest venture is the Collaborative Experience, Inc., a life empowerment company with business partner Toni Coleman Brown. As publishers, they have compiled a series of Amazon bestselling books and created the opportunity for more than fifty writers to become published co-authors. The series includes *Delayed But Not Denied 1: 20 Stories about Life and Resiliency*, published in 2016, followed by *Delayed But Not Denied 2: Real Stories about Hope, Faith and Triumph*, published in *2017*. *Delayed But Not Denied 3: Real People Sharing Stories About Healing and Growth*, was released in fall 2018.

As a freelance publicist , Shaw's client list included Iyana Vansant, Michael Biased, Circle of Sisters Expo, and the International African Arts Festival, to name a few. Julia consults with the National Black Writers Conference, the Small Business Bootcamp for Women, *The Network Journal Magazine*'s 40 Under Forty Achievement Awards, and the 25 Influential Women in Business Awards.

Julia is a contributing author to the Amazon bestseller Network to Increase Your Net Worth, compiled by Toni Coleman Brown, and she was featured in *Stepping' Out with Attitude: Sister, Sell your Dream* by Anita Buckley. She serves as director of the Rockdale Village Community Center and is a dazzling Paparazzi Jewelry consultant. The proud mother of two daughters and the grandmother of three, she resides in Queens, New York.

Email:	collaborativeexperience@gmail.com
Website:	www.delayedbutnotdenied.info www.thecollaborativeexperience.com
LinkedIn:	julia_d_shaw1
Facebook:	juliadshaw1 meettheauthorexperience
Twitter:	@juliadshaw1

SINGLE MOMS RISE! OVERCOMING THE EMOTIONAL CHALLENGES OF BEING A SINGLE PARENT

By Julia D. Shaw

The word "love" can be used as a noun or verb, and thus it has many meanings. As a noun, it can mean "warm attachment, enthusiasm, or devotion." As a verb, love means "to like or desire actively, take pleasure in." We have different perceptions of love and how to show love to others. To love and to be loved is the catalyst of many life dramas. In the quest for true love, I, like others, have had my heart broken once or twice. It is an unavoidable experience in the saga of love. In my life, I have cried many tears in the name of love.

When I think back to my childhood, I remember escaping my reality by siting up late at night watching Doris Day and Rock Hudson movies on TV. The theme of all the movies was boy meets girl. Girl plays hard to get. Then boy pursues girl until she gives in, they fall in love, and they live happily ever after. That's how I thought my story was going to go when I fell in love with Gregory Smith. He lived across the street from my aunt's house. He sat on his front steps, and I sat on my aunt's back porch, and we stared across the street at each other. In our minds, it was love at first sight. We were boyfriend and girlfriend during the summer of Marvin Gaye's hit singles "Let's Get It On" and "Sexual Healing." We hung out with two other teen couples in Frankie's back yard. Gregory was my first love; we hugged and kissed, but we never had the opportunity to be alone to do anything else. It was an awesome summer. We had so much fun until Mark informed me that Gregory was messing around with this girl Carmen. Word on the street was they were "doing it." I was crushed! My heart was broken in the name of love. With tear-filled eyes, I broke up with him. I could not understand why this was happening to me. This wasn't how it when down in the movies. This may sound a bit naïve, but I had been watching Doris and Rock for years. In my fifteen-year-old mind, that was the way relationships were supposed to go.

Fast-forward ten years. It was never my plan to have not one, but two baby daddies. The second one was also my husband, who I thought was my life partner. In my mind, we were going to build a life together, especially since our daughter was born four days short of our being married for exactly nine months! I believed him when he said, "Julia, I love you!" I was the chosen one. He wanted to be with me. He wanted to marry me, not his other daughter's mother, not the chick whose panties I found in his laundry while washing our clothes. And, yes, he married me! But everything changed the moment we said "I do." I couldn't understand why he cheated and lied to me. Why did he creep around behind my back with my new so-called friend from the neighborhood who came in and out of my house? Why was he so mean to me while I was pregnant with his child? I would pack up my kids, leaving him and going to my mother's house again and again. I did this about ten times. Each time, he would come and get me and I would go back.

I got tired of the rollercoaster ride in the name of love and family. I was miserable and couldn't take it anymore. The last time I left, I refused to come back. I cried for three weeks straight until my tear ducts were dry. They couldn't produce any more water, not a drop. That was the sign to stop crying and pull myself together. I had two babies depending on only me. How did I get here? Why am I here? I am a good person. I'm a nice person. He told me that he loved me, told me that cared. I believed him! Then why was I broken hearted and alone? I didn't understand why! The pain inside was crippling. THIS WAS NEVER MY PLAN!

For years, I lived in a quasi-zombie state of existence, giving off the image of a strong Black woman on the outside, but inside, I was emotionally dead. I felt like a lost, angry little girl left alone in the role of the mother and father taking care of my two daughters. I was depressed, overwhelmed, and on a quest for emotional survival, all while struggling financially with very little child support. I was a hot mess! I existed day to day with no answers to my questions, no plans for my future, no solutions to my problems, and no definable goals. Wondering how I had gotten there consumed me.

The shift in my life came when I STOPPED dwelling on the unchangeable past and began to focus on how to move forward. It wasn't easy, but I did it!

My goal in this chapter is to share my strategies for taking control of my reality and changing my destiny.

First, I had to stop living the role of a victim and get the victim mentality out of my head. I had to step back and look at the facts—not my dreams of love and happiness, but the reality of the one-sided relationship I chose to be in. There were actions that didn't match the words "I love you" long before any babies were born. I called these actions little red flags that I couldn't see because I was so busy showing them I was a loving girlfriend and wife. I was always going above and beyond to prove my love, so I couldn't see the little red flags until they became big red flags hitting me over the head. Letting go of the victim mindset gave me the clarity to forgive myself. I accepted my choices, I owned them, and now I am going to do my best to make better choices as I move into my greatness.

My negative feelings and emotions of self-doubt and resentment were like poison to my already broken heart. Anger and disappointment hit me like a bolt of lightning and were hard to overcome. It wasn't right, and it wasn't fair. My daughters' fathers had gone on with their lives and had not lived up to their promised responsibilities as parents. I didn't realize the depth of my anger until my sister said I was verbally abusive to my children. They didn't deserve to feel my pain. The last thing in the world I wanted to do was add to the trauma they felt as fatherless little girls. I asked for God's help and guidance: "Please, give me the strength to heal my heart. Please, show me how to be a better mother to my children." My shift continued. I consciously began to catch thoughts of anger when they entered my mind and replace them with thoughts of how blessed I was to have intelligent, beautiful, and healthy children. I told myself it was their loss, not mine. They were going to miss out on seeing our daughters grow up—a once-in-a-lifetime experience. My prayers for the strength and guidance to be a good mother to my children are ongoing and continue into their adulthood.

It's true that it takes a village to raise a child. Although I am a single mom, I didn't raise my children alone. With the support of family and friends, I was able to create a loving and stable environment for my children as they grew up. Words can't describe the love, appreciation, and gratitude I have for my mother's hands-on support and assistance to me while raising the girls. She dropped them off and picked them up from the daycare center. She babysat for days when I had to travel for business and even read bedtime stories. I am truly blessed to have Letha Shaw as my mom.

My village included a host of friends that I loved and trusted. Mzee Moyo and Anita Herring were mentors and friends who gave me advice on many aspects of life, but what I valued most was their insights on parenting. Both were older than me with adult children, and they willingly shared their experiences. They also told me the cold, hard facts about what I was doing right or wrong when dealing with my children. They were the wise elders in my village, but they passed away many years ago. I miss them dearly, but their words of wisdom are with me today and I share them with others. I had a host of friends who came into my life when I needed them most and helped me with my children—but Cary, my best friend, and Kelly, a true godmother, were my babysitting team that held me down, and I appreciate them. As a single mom, you must create a village of family and friends who are willing to help you with your children. Always let them know you appreciate their support.

They say that hindsight is 20/20. As I look back at the mistakes I made as a parent, the one that stands out most in my mind is that wish I was more engaged with my children. There are six years between my daughters, so to keep them from fighting when we went out, each child would bring a friend or two. I always had a car full of kids. That was great; they had fun. For example, when we went to the pool during the summer, they would be in the pool having fun and I would be sitting in a lounge chair doing paperwork, working on my budget, or writing my grocery list. I was there but not engaged, not creating memories, not living in the moment, not having fun with my children. I can't change the past—it is what it is—but now I am very engaged with my grandchildren. We paint and draw, we go to the park, and we go to the movies! We have fun—we are creating great memories! When I chat with busy parents, I share my views on the importance of engagement with their children and other young family members.

Single moms are focused! We are intense because we have a lot going on! Taking care of the kids, paying the bills, cooking, cleaning, taking the kids to activities like basketball, dance, tutoring, music lessons, birthday parties, holidays, school plays, Girl Scouts—you name it, we are doing it for our children.

What about ME, my wants, my needs, my dreams and goals? How do I make myself happy? What about my love life? In the mix of being Mom, how do I do me? I remember praying for fifteen minutes of uninterrupted thought. The bathroom was my haven for peace until the door knob jiggled, followed by a loud knock on the door if it was locked. "Mommy what you doing? Can I come in?" My personal needs were on the back burner of the stove. I had to figure out ways create my personal happiness. My faith in God was a great comfort in the hardest times. From time to time, I hung out with my friends, went to conferences, socialized, and went out on dates. It was important to create a little "Julia time." I also wrote my thoughts and feelings in journals. It was an emotional and creative way to release stress. Single motherhood was hard. I made a lot of sacrifices for my children, but it was my choice, and I don't regret it.

Now, I am on the other side of motherhood. My daughters are grown and on their own. It wasn't easy, but it has been worth every minute. I am proud to be a single mom! I am proud of my daughters. I have a rich, full life and wouldn't change it for anything! My experiences in life empowered me to grow and love myself unconditionally. Did I make mistakes? Yes, and when I did, I was never too proud to apologize to my daughters. I would say, "I am doing the best I can. You were not born with a how-to manual, so I am learning as we live our lives together."

Now, I understand the importance of all my successes and struggles. Know that if I can help anyone by sharing my experiences, I will. It is important for me to help others because there were so many who helped me as I traveled on my life journey as a single parent. I want to a make a difference in the lives of others, to share my passion for positive change with a purpose to encourage and help others on their life journey. I have overcome the drama of being a single mom, endured the pain, released the negative emotions, and continue to heal as I grow!

ABOUT
Janette "Justice" Carter

Janette "Justice" Carter's positive demeanor never wanes. She supports several organizations and is vested in community engagement and social causes. Justice shares her message of empowerment as a motivational speaker and a co-author in the *Delayed But Not Denied* book series. Janette B. Carter speaks candidly on topics such as leadership, overcoming obstacles, and personal development. In this capacity, she enlightens, educates, and empowers individuals, professional organizations, and groups of all ages. Her heartfelt presentations include stories that inspire her audiences to strategize, organize, and act.

In January 2016, she was appointed America's Plus-size professional model and spokesperson by eMediaCampaigns! Carter started with Gold Canyon Candles in October 2011 and has been booming in her business. Her charismatic demeanor has drawn people to her in a magnitude that's so massive, it's no wonder she's a team leader.

She retired from the NYC Department of Corrections in September 2014. She is also a mother of three adult children and grandmother to eight.

Facebook: Janette "Justice" Carter

Instagram: justusscents

THE HAPPY RETIREMENT

By Janette "Justice" Carter

I was once a correctional officer who worked on Riker's Island until there was a knock on my door one very hot summer afternoon while I was cleaning the house. My dogs were barking loudly, so before going to the door I looked out the window and saw a van from the Department of Corrections. My heart started racing. As I opened the door, my heart sank to my toes because I knew what this visit was about.

"Good afternoon. May I help you?" I said to the officers. The captain and the officer explained what the visit was for and what they needed to collect from me. I was being terminated from a job that I had worked for nineteen years. The captain was upset. He clearly didn't want to take the shield and ID card. But I invited them in, we had a great conversation, and at the end of the chat, I gave them what they came for. They wished me well as I let them out the door. As I closed the front door, the world that I had known for all those years abruptly came to an end. I was scared, mad, and confused. But mostly, I was relieved.

All kinds of thoughts were racing in my head, but the one that stood out most in my mind was *where do I go from here?* Being fired from the Department of Corrections meant that I would not be entitled to my pension or my medical benefits, both of which I had worked very hard for. My benefits were the reason I took the damn job in the first place. But working there wasn't safe, and as a result I ended up suffering several injuries. Those injuries required surgeries, which caused me to miss a lot of work. And that caused me to be unjustifiably terminated.

That night, I struggled to sleep. It felt like the longest night of my entire life. I prayed, cried, and sat up in my bed thinking about what I was going to do. It was like I was in a big fog. I didn't know how I was going to maintain my home. I thought about my obligations to my children and grandchildren. And every time I thought about it, I just kept coming back to the word "fired." And all I could think was, "How could they do this to me?"

It was a Friday when the officers arrived on my doorstep, so my entire weekend was filled with uncertainty. Yet ironically, I felt relieved. What happened next is what I think any human would do. I panicked! But I knew what I needed to do. I made a list of every account that I had where I knew I could withdraw money. I sat down and said, "Father God, as sure as I am that you are the head of my life, I know that this is not the end. It is the beginning of something great." Over the course of the next three years, my life would change forever.

The next day, I got still and quiet. I shut the noise out of my head, and I thought, "What would my mother do?" That is when this peace began to come over me and I realized that the fighter that I am had prepared me for this moment in my life. The fighter in me took over. I started making payment arrangements with every account that I had. I explained to them that all I owed would eventually be paid, but I needed a payment plan with the minimum amount of money as possible. I had good credit, which is how I was able to secure most of my accounts with minimum payments. I also had a lucrative candle business, which had to become my number-one source of income.

My lawyers did their very best to have the Department of Corrections reinstate my disability, which gave me a third of my pension. Most people cannot even survive on half of their pension, let alone a third. But the God that I serve promised me that He would make my enemies my footstool. After winning my case with the New York City Employees' Retirement System, it was time to fight Social Security Disability. That was a battle, but it wasn't my battle. God won that case with the help of my lawyers.

During this entire ordeal, I was in much pain. I required four surgeries. I'm still fighting with Worker's Compensation to approve more surgeries. The most serious surgery I needed was a knee replacement. A fall I took in 2013 shattered my knee, and from that day until August 13, 2018, I was in constant pain. Once again, my God and my lawyers won that battle, and I got the approval to have my surgery in August of this year. After that surgery, my life changed again. I never lost my hope, and I never stopped believing that I would one day be happy in my retirement.

I have always been an encouraging person, and I have always encouraged women to do better and want better in life. Now I teach them how to prepare for retirement, as I am living proof that you can have a happy retirement. Today, being happy is my number-one priority. Yes, God comes first and my family comes next, but if I'm not happy, none of that really matters to me.

Retirement in and of itself is a dichotomy of sorts. On the one hand, it's something that most retirees-to-be can't wait for. The final day at their workplace can't come fast enough. On the other hand, the reality of what typically is the end of an era may make one feel more daunted than daring. What I do know for sure is that the Happy Retirement includes components that reflect who you are. It involves all things that make you thrive.

For example, as often as you can, participate in activities that confirm your purpose and bring you joy. Maybe you played softball for forty-five years. If you are still able, then keep playing. There are no shortages of senior league softball teams. If you enjoyed social outings while working, you will have more opportunities to spend time with your friends and associates, and you should do that. Anything that keeps you stimulated and helps you grow and prosper should be a consistent part of your life.

In retirement, you may not know exactly what to do. You may find yourself missing coworkers, or you may feel a decreased sense of purpose. But all these things are a part of it. Many retirees are generally happy about the transition. Others—even those who appear to have it all—struggle to find happiness. But it doesn't have to be that way.

A Happy Retirement doesn't happen because of one's background or privileges. It happens because the retiree does what he or she believes happiness is. Happiness for me includes, getting up at six a.m. for prayer, then pouring positive affirmations into my grandson before he starts his day or taking my granddaughter to Pre-K and singing all the songs she likes along the way. These things are absolutely priceless to me. Anything that I set in motion with the intent to elevate my life and others usually results in incredible bliss. Retirement is a great time to execute your own happiness, habits, and life decisions. You should enjoy every single day of your retirement, knowing that each one can be valuable and exciting.

I have truly embraced my new lifestyle—The Happy Retirement! All the time I spent working on Riker's Island next to LGA Airport, I would always hear the planes and imagine myself being on them traveling places. I never stop dreaming about that. Today, I get on more airplanes than I ever have in my life. My dream as a little girl of going places on planes has actually come true! I have flown first-class to Barcelona to cruise the Mediterranean Sea. I have been to many Caribbean islands plenty of times by air and by ship, and I am loving it. At first, I didn't know how I was going to make it financially, but by paying myself first and savings, I did it and you can, too.

Fast-forward to this wonderful fall day. As I am leaving church, I can hear my feet crunching the leaves. I look up into the sky, and I thank my Heavenly Father. I smile and begin to skip like a little girl because I am happy. Happy to be retired. And happy to be living my life on purpose, enjoying each and every day. It hasn't always been this way. Nevertheless, I thank God that now it is.

ABOUT
Dionely Reyes

Dionely Reyes blends humor, music, and stories to inspire and motivate in both English and Spanish on the radio and via her social media accounts on Facebook, YouTube, and Instagram @didinspire. After immigrating with her family from the Dominican Republic as a young girl, she learned English quickly, excelled in school, and received her college education from Rutgers University and Thomas Edison State University. As the daughter of business owners and a community leader, Dionely was raised to think outside the box and with an understanding that success is not only based on how far you go, but on how much you help others along the way. Her parents inspired her by the way they lived their lives as they rose from living in a small village in a developing country in the Caribbean, to uprooting the family and moving to one of the most dangerous cities in the United States, to finally moving to the suburbs, all while keeping the family together. Just like she and her siblings were her parents' motivation, Dionely's son is her motivation. She enjoyed working in real estate, but her vocation is in helping people be the best version of themselves. After surviving gaslighting, Dionely gained a greater understanding of what it takes to overcome adversity and is thriving doing what she loves.

Email:	didinspire@gmail.com
Instagram:	@didinspire
YouTube:	didinspire
Facebook:	didinspire
Website:	www.didinspire.com

SURVIVING GASLIGHTING: LIVING YOUR TRUTH

By Dionely Reyes

I didn't realize gaslighting was a thing until I lived through it. It was brought to my attention by a loved one, and once I did my research, I realized it was exactly what had been happening to me. The term "gaslighting" originates from the 1938 Patrick Hamilton play Gaslight and its 1940 and 1944 film adaptations, where the husband gradually made his wife believe she is insane so he could steal from her. He isolated her from everyone and began to manipulate the lighting in their home. When the wife would ask him if he noticed the difference in the lighting, he would deny it and tell her she was imagining it. Living in isolation and having no other point of reference, the wife believed she was going insane. But she wasn't—she was being conned by her husband.

A true gaslighter will attempt to keep you off balance and not knowing what to expect so you have no option but to rely on them for any sense of stability. This type of manipulation often comes from someone you consider a friend, a boss, a coworker, a family member, or a romantic partner. It's usually someone you hold in high regard and who has influence in your life. I dealt with two very influential swindlers who came into my life at the same time and fed off each other by corroborating their lies. These people had one goal in mind, and that was to keep me in a constant state of confusion and dependency. They tried to rewire my thinking with negative validation by privately and repeatedly saying things to me like "you are weak," "you will never make it without me," "you are trash," and "you are mentally unstable." They would repeat this over and over and over until it became a sort of mantra in my mind.

After saying these things to me, they would follow up with very public nice gestures to keep me confused emotionally. This is commonly called "love bombing," which is where you're showered with gifts, compliments, and public displays of affection. Obviously, this would create confusion. I would think to myself, "They're being so nice to me now; maybe they didn't mean to be as cruel as they were." I would let my guard down and feel like I could be vulnerable again, and they would later use this against me. I eventually came to understand these gestures were not sincere. They were tactics to deceive me into feeling like I was forever indebted to them and like I needed to prove my unconditional love and appreciation by obeying and not complaining about the verbal abuse. I realized that even if I behaved exactly how they wanted me to behave, I would never gain their approval.

When I brought up a concern, they refused to validate it but instead would respond with outrageous claims and incendiary comments about my family and me to divert the conversation away from my original concern and force me to defend myself against this new allegation or comment. They clearly were trying to wear me down and make me feel like I was crazy or wrong, to the point where I would end up apologizing. My emotions were often dismissed as me being "too sensitive" or "that never happened…you're imagining it," and, finally, "you are mentally unstable." When I stood up for myself, they would go as far as to call my family to try to convince them that I was going nuts. My family and friends knew better because they had witnessed the lies and manipulation, but they left it up to me to realize it for myself and decide to leave the situation. My biggest mistake was believing the lies they told about themselves, about other people, and about me.

They tried hard to drive a wedge between my loved ones and me by playing us against each other with lies. They would frequently refer to my disagreements with my family and friends to remind me that I had no one else to count on except them. They would constantly tell me that they defended me when my loved ones spoke poorly about me behind my back. At one point, my loved ones became concerned and reached out to me because I no longer looked like my normal happy self, and it didn't make sense why I had to ask for permission to do things that adults should be free to do. It was clear to them that something seemed off. But my manipulators response to me was that my family and friends were jealous and didn't really love me; then they would refer back to disagreements I'd had with them. My support system didn't understand why I kept believing their lies, but I felt like I was trapped.

One day, I finally reached a breaking point when all the contradictory comments, verbal abuse, and threats were getting to me. I felt like I was going crazy. I had been walking on eggshells for too long. My manipulators made me feel like even God didn't love me and that He would punish me in the worst way if I continued to disobey their wishes. They wanted me to feel like they were the only source of power in my life. But on this particular Sunday, I did something I hadn't done in a while: with tears in my eyes, I looked up and prayed "God, help me!" Suddenly, I felt a strong urge to call one of my dearest friends who would randomly call to pray for me and remind me to "remember to get in touch with God" and that I have a higher calling. Even though I would find it strange, I knew it came from a place of love. That day, I called her, crying and said, "I want to go to your church with you."

The cons viewed this as an act of defiance, but my mind was made up and I went. I cried the entire time I was at church. And when I heard the pastor speak, I felt something I had not felt in so long—a sense of relief and peace. At that moment, I knew everything would be all right if I just trusted God. From that point on, my perspective started to change, and I slowly but surely started seeing the truth behind the lies. Immediately when I got back from church, they accused me of lying about going to church. They assured me that they had witnesses who saw me somewhere else having fun and that they took pictures and videos of me in the act! I was shocked and bewildered, but I realized they were conniving liars. I started to second-guess everything they said from that point on. My eyes were finally open.

This was the turning point. I started to see things for what they were. I followed my urge to reach out to my loved ones, and they recommended I read certain books. I started to infuse my mind with facts. One of the first books I read was Robert Greene's *48 Laws of Power*, from which I learned different strategies that were being used to manipulate me and realized how deadly isolation from my support system was. I started to reach out to more of my loved ones. This was my first step toward freedom. I then realized that the only solution was for me to break away from my manipulators. Before these individuals came into my life, I was joyful, independent, and enjoyed being on radio shows. I never thought that a college-educated woman like me would fall for psychological manipulation, but I did.

After praying for many nights, I experienced a paradigm shift and decided to leave. All it took was for me to make the firm decision to leave, and God aligned everyone and everything so that I could do it. I took a leap of faith. Suddenly, my questions like "Where will I go?" "What will I do?" "Where will I work?" and "What will I drive?" were all answered. I made a promise to God that if I made it through, I would make it my purpose to show others the way to survive and thrive.

Leaving wasn't easy. They tried to stop me—not because they loved me, but because they wanted to keep controlling me. To them, my leaving on my own terms was like a slave leaving a slave owner. They didn't see me as a human being; they saw me as property. They did things like trying to block my exit by threatening to harm me. They even went as far as recording me and blocking out the things they said to try to use it against me. But I understood that there was nothing they could do to me that was greater than God's grace.

They promised to ruin my life if I ever told my testimony, but this is not about them. This is about keeping my promise to God. If, after reading this, you discover that you or someone you know is going through a similar situation, please understand the best option is to leave as soon as possible. The resources are out there to assist. I am not a psychologist, but I am someone who lived through it, survived it, and am thriving after it, and you or they can, too.

Reading books can help. Reading *The Four Agreements* by Don Miguel Ruiz helped me understand that my self-worth cannot be based on what others say about me. I realized that I could no longer waste my energy arguing and defending myself against lies. After I read *The Secret* and studied the law of attraction and the power of visualization, everything that I saw in my future was attracted to me. Keeping a journal helped me keep track of events and sort through the lies. Also, listen to music. I enjoy listening to Dembow. It can help keep you uplifted.

Martin Luther King, Jr. said, *"Darkness cannot drive out darkness; only light can do that. Hate cannot drive out hate; only love can do that."* I learned to forgive my gaslighters. I pray for them and wish them well. I refuse to allow people to ruin my kind heart and soul. I understand that hurt people hurt people, and it is not my job to hurt or heal them. I am focusing on me and living my truth, which is that I deserve to be treated with love, dignity, and respect.

ABOUT
Kathleen Greely

Kathleen Greely is a proven visionary leader, a fundraising professional, and a graduate of Spring Arbor University. Prior to her private sector experience, Kathleen developed an extensive background in dealing with youth and families through public education and training programs. She acquired skills in community building and economic and workforce development in private and non-profit work environments, including a twenty-plus-year commitment to social and civic engagement. Kathleen created and coordinated workforce development strategies that resulted in more than 2,000 jobs and training opportunities for unemployed residents in northwest Ohio.

After many years in Ohio, Kathleen decided to make a change and move to the West Coast. As Director of Marketing for an Oakland Bay-area law firm, she focused on tax-deferred exchanges. She managed partnership agreements with real estate brokers, CPAs, financial advisors, and local chambers of commerce. As an expert in tax-deferred exchanges, she often conducted seminars and presentations on the subject on the West Coast and in cities throughout the U.S.

With a passion for helping others, Kathleen prides herself on taking time to understand her clients' immediate and long-term goals. She is an executive board member of Cancer Connection of Northwest Ohio and a non-Hodgkin's lymphoma cancer survivor. Currently, she is the President/CEO of Broken Crayons Still Coloring, LLC in northwest Ohio.

Twitter:	@StillColoringU
	@KhatGhurl
Facebook:	Kathleen Kathleen (personal page)
Facebook:	Conquering Lymphoma with kathleen@BrokenCrayonsStillColoring

BROKEN CRAYONS STILL COLORING

By Kathleen Greely

The journey through chemotherapy was arduous and lonely for me. People scattered like roaches when you turn the lights on after I shared my diagnosis. Even family members chose not to call to support me, let alone close friends...or people I thought were close friends.

I shared the news with my supervisor (who shared with me that they, too, were a cancer survivor). Yet somehow after my disclosure suddenly, there was no money available for my position and I was terminated within a week. Now I was left with no friends, no work, no money, and limited contact with family members. I was blessed to have one sister come up to Detroit to sit with me during chemotherapy. My mother did call to check in weekly.

How could this be? Health and well-being have always been aspects of my daily life—where did I go wrong? My daily workouts and green drinks were consistent. I had been living my life with intention—a subservient leader, a successful career in community building and consumer advocacy—impacting the lives of so many youth, families, and seniors for so many years. Being of service is something I have found worthwhile and most enjoyable, but on August 30, 2016, my life changed drastically. This was the day I was diagnosed with stage 3 follicular non-Hodgkin's lymphoma at the age of 57. After I experienced immense pain in my face from a lump just under and behind my ear, tests showed cancer in my face, neck, chest, stomach, and back. I went from being completely healthy to being devastated with the news that I was facing a health crisis that would force me to fight for my life. All I could think about was how glad I was that I had gotten a new life insurance policy approved before I was diagnosed. I had not a clue where my spiritual journey was taking me next.

With a heavy heart and complete trust in God's healing power, I embraced this difficult journey that started with hardcore chemotherapy within one week of my biopsy. Along with my journey of healing, I was consistently being challenged with mounting medical expenses, out-of-pocket fees, and prescription costs. Then with my job assignment ending due to lack of funding (but we know what was really going on there) only added to my daily stress.

Although this diagnosis completely turned my life upside down, it also prompted me to focus on the universal law of giving and receiving: **the law of reciprocity**. I began to ask myself—where am I not giving? How can I manifest a fruitful life, despite the fact that I may be transitioning from this life? There was still this innate feeling that God was trying to communicate new possibility through me and that it was important to stay spiritually aligned if I was ever to make it safely beyond this current moment and to the other side of remission. I felt broken, yet I still desired to create a color-filled life from where I stood—as a spiritual being living a human experience of cancer survivorship. Manifesting a high level of energy and enhancing my vibration through my thoughts, emotions and my actions, I began to create possibility from nothing. I was like broken crayons still coloring.

The cancer treatment center that administered my chemotherapy was not very user friendly, and I had slipped through the cracks at a very critical time. I remember the first day of my treatment. No one had told me to bring a lunch and that I would be there all day. I later went to the area where food was sold in the hospital, but it was only fast food—unhealthy food choices. The restaurant next door did have hot soup, but it was filled with sodium, and other food items that were packed with preservatives and partially hydrogenated oils. If I wanted healthier food items, I had to walk all the way across campus. As a cancer patient with very low energy, that was difficult. I grew concerned and was disenchanted about the treatment I had received. There were no healthy food choices, and there was no orientation to let me know that I could have prepared a healthy meal for the day. **All I could think of was the importance of advocacy for oneself.**

Of course, I complained. The Director of Public Relations, reached out to offer an apology. They were open to suggestions and admitted to falling short in this area of service. I asked if I could sell fresh fruit, vegetables, and nuts to the many patients who were being seen, maybe three days a week. They engaged me in conversation but later said I couldn't do it because the hospital administration required that food come packaged, not prepared by me. They kept communication open with me, and I was encouraged to call if I wanted help with launching a program that could serve cancer survivors in the future. They expressed an appreciation for the way in which I advocated for myself. I received a follow-up letter and two phone calls because they liked my ideas, and they offered to help me start a cancer survivorship program. It was a pleasant interaction, but at that time, my work/life balance was becoming complex.

I was well into my treatment and still did not have a social worker assigned to me. Bills were piling up, and I didn't know how I was going to pay rent. Here I was, a workforce development guru with an understanding of health and human services—but knew nothing about being in the state of Michigan as a stage 3 cancer patient. I did not have a point of reference for cancer survivorship and how to prepare for a worst-case scenario. I was still without the resources necessary to pay rent. And I didn't get an appointment to meet with the social worker until November, but by then eviction was staring me in the face. How had I become a near-homeless cancer patient?

Before I knew it, the Christmas season was upon me. Moved to share by the spirit of the season, I created Conquering Lymphoma with Kathleen, a GoFundMe/Facebook page to help ease the financial strain of fighting cancer. I was devastated, but I was humbled and compelled to ask others to consider giving a gift of thanks in honor of all the community leaders and youth and senior advocates they may have known. Donations came in from across the country: from my BFFs in the Bay Area and in central and southern California, from business associates, strangers, a few family members, extended family members, and friends. Those donations did, in fact, go toward medical expenses, out-of-pocket fees, prescription and travel costs, and anything else I needed. It's incredibly humbling to be in a position where you need the help of friends, relatives, colleagues, and even strangers to get the medical treatment needed to survive!

Through networking, I discovered that my cancer treatment center had a facility in Oakland County, where I lived, and that I qualified for services there as well. I attended classes and workshops and developed a relationship with the social worker in that facility, which was how I was able to pay for two months' rent. She made sure the check was in my name. I knew then that this lady knew what I was up against. She introduced me to other coordinators of cancer survivorship programs and services, and it was then that I began to find a "new" tribe. Those who were leading the conversation of cancer survivorship in the southeast Michigan area took a liking to me, and I, too, enjoyed these new relationships. Meditating and praying in gratitude for my "new" network, I kept asking the question—where am I not giving? How can I manifest a fruitful life, in spite of the fact that I may be transitioning from this life?

Eviction was still fast approaching. Because of my meeting with the social worker in November, I got the help I needed to complete my paperwork to receive Social Security. It helped, of course, but it was not enough to live on. I still had to go to eviction court—and I lost. So, after the PET scan indicated that I was in remission, I had to find a place to live. I chose to move to Ohio, closer to family, because I was unsure about the stability of my health.

The next challenge reared its head as soon I arrived in Ohio—my car stopped working. OMG! It had been more than twenty years since I'd been without my own car. This created a dilemma for me because I did not have a healthy relationship with my family. It felt somewhat humiliating, yet divine all at the same time. I could feel the energy around me shifting to "Be still and know that I Am." I remained mindful of and present to what I really wanted—healing. It was time for stillness, gratitude, selfishness—it was time for remission. It was time to be still. When I looked at my health, wealth, relationship with self, and integrity, I discovered that my capacity to live my life on purpose was out of balance. Spiritually, I was ready to experience a deeper peace.

I asked: What is my spiritual connection to being in Ohio? I have only experienced pain and heartache in Ohio. How will I serve? Pema Chödrön, an American Tibetan Buddhist, ordained nun, and author, teaches that nothing goes away until it has taught us what we need to know. So, I stayed in meditation and prayer. I asked myself the question: What am I here in Ohio to learn? What is it that I need to know? Who do I need to be? I began to see being in Ohio as my opportunity to heal: an opportunity to access healing energy and healthy resources flowing seamlessly and effortlessly into my life. I began to see being in Ohio as my opportunity to have a loving relationship with my family.

One morning, before going into my five o'clock meditation, I asked the Divine to help me with my brain fog (chemo brain). I wanted to recollect some of what I had done in the past week, but for the life of me, I could not recall everything. My thinking was blurred. This was disturbing to me because I had always relied on my mental and physical assets, and both seemed to be dwindling. I began to think again about my being in Ohio, and I wondered what I was supposed to do about my ability to recall from one moment to the next. After my meditation, I sat at the kitchen table drinking my tea and watching a cardinal land on my patio. I thanked God for a place to be; my life wasn't perfect, but I was thankful for what I did have. The next thing I knew, I received a call from a cancer survivors retreat facility off the western peninsula in Michigan inviting me to come stay for the weekend. I explained that I was now living in northwest Ohio and that my car wasn't working. The owner and executive director, Renee, said, "Kathleen, I really like you and have been impressed by your tenacious spirit. I'll tell you what we'll do—we will rent a vehicle for you so you can attend the retreat this weekend." I was so excited! Inspired! Thoroughly impressed, I did everything I could to get to the retreat. This is perfect, I thought. This is in alignment with how I do life—reassessing and recalibrating my life during a retreat!

I spoke with my brother, who agreed to support me with the amount of money needed to rent the vehicle (because Renee had agreed to reimburse me). But since I'd just relocated to Ohio and had not yet changed my identification, I still had Michigan ID, no major credit card, and an Ohio address—and the driver's license and address had to match up. Even though the cost would be covered, I had to make it doable on the front end. Like I mentioned, reimbursement was imminent, and I could give my brother his money right back! This was something they had never done before, but I couldn't get it done. I asked God why this opportunity was being presented to me. This is what I do—retreats. This seemed like a perfect solution…yet it wasn't.

As I mentioned, I was not in healthy relationships with my family. I was feeling some kind of way about having to ask for help, especially from "them." Instead of continually feeling humiliated, though, I manifested a different response through my meditation—**Family is primary**. That kept coming up for me. I began to extend an olive branch, especially to those to whom I felt the strongest aversion. Realizing that "heart" work is hard work, I understood that if I was to begin to heal, I needed to lean in to my fear of not being loved and supported by my family. This meant letting go of the shame, blame, and resentment I held toward my siblings for shunning me. I needed to let go of my resistance to showing up at family gatherings and to stop hiding what

I really wanted—love and acceptance. I wanted to forgive my family, but I needed to forgive myself first. Daily mindfulness meditation was necessary.

Days later, it occurred to me to call each of my family members and admit that I was angry and shortsighted and that we were not speaking because I was holding on to anger. I further explained that I wanted to bridge the gap, and I asked them to join me in my effort to clean up the toxic energy in our relationship. Instead of making them wrong, I took ownership of my anger and what I was feeling. Choosing to be a light—to be the cause in the matter of healing myself in relation to my family—I created a Mother's Day event. I invited my siblings, my nieces and nephews, and my first cousins and their kids to come over and bring a piece of the soul our mothers left behind: their recipes! I asked them, "What did your Momma make that you can't live without, so you make it better than anyone else in the family?" I had more than seventy guests! What a joy-filled event it was. My sister Patricia even flew in from Florida {smiles}.

I made a commitment to attend every event hosted by my family that year, even though it was hard sometimes to sit with family that I thought had little love for me. I left early once to deal with the heartache of being treated like my prayer wasn't acceptable because I study Tibetan Buddhism. The family politics were sometimes unbearable. But I was committed to my personal and spiritual journey…committed to eradicating cancer from my body and from the most intimate relationships in my life. I am committed to truth, balance, order, and harmony in my life, and therefore, I am the cause in the matter of my heart being as light as a feather.

In an attempt to build my trust in others, I reached out to a few old high school friends and began to share my journey as a cancer survivor. People were very supportive. My high school friend Patrice was willing to help me with the money needed to get my electricity turned on. My dear friend Marva helped me to focus on health and human services so I could keep food stamps and healthcare going. My caseworker in Michigan was helpful by ensuring everything transferred to Ohio. Another friend helped me to make my life insurance payments. I was able to eat well with $194 a month in food stamps, and I borrowed my sister's car to make it to all my doctor's appointments. When I found out I qualified for transportation through my healthcare, I used Lyft. I kept asking God that question: "Why am I here?" Remembering that there is a reason for everything, I knew that the answer would only come through spiritual awareness or awakening. I embraced the current season of my life. **"Be still and know that I Am."**

I let myself laugh at the confusion, kept smiling through the tears, and reminded myself that everything happens for a reason. It was then that I realized I always seemed to be in Ohio when it was time for personal and spiritual growth. That's when I asked the Divine, "What is it that is incomplete?" Then it occurred to me that this was about completion. It wasn't about using old tools in a new way or sitting around talking about what wasn't working. I have completed so many leadership trainings and coaching programs and have written blueprints for workforce development, business development, education, and training. When you provide that level of teaching, it requires you to do the work yourself. This time, it was about focusing on my self-development. This time in Ohio was about me making a personal commitment to myself during this leg of my life journey. I had to hold on to my healing energy because in order to soar, I had to re-learn F.L.Y.—**First Love Yourself.**

The thought began to fill my mental space like a white light—I would return to college after more than fourteen years and complete my degree. I only needed a class or two to finish. Furthermore, thinking critically would exercise my mental muscles. Expressive writing would help me to minimize chemo brain... I could still be a promise in the world while conquering lymphoma. It occurred to me that it was time to create my own personal retreat, just for me. I had done thirty-day silent meditation retreats at home before. They had manifested great things, but for other people and their businesses. **This season, these broken crayons would be coloring for my benefit and edification.** When cancer shows up, it means your life is calling. Inspiration exists, but it has to find you working! My friend Asara Tsehai, author and founder of A Touch of Life, said it best: "You are your own medicine."

One might ask why I would choose to return to college to complete a degree after more than fourteen years away when I was in remission from incurable cancer and on permanent disability. My response is because thinking critically helped me to exercise my mental musculature. It not only demonstrated self-love and perseverance, but I was able to figure out how cancer can translate into careers. With the help of my academic advisor, I was able to structure my coursework to complete a feasibility study on cancer survivorship programs for northwest Ohio. Because I completed that study, I was able to submit an application for a grant to start my own cancer survivorship retreat series—a viable business model significant to the healing and skills development of cancer survivors. Based on my initial investigation into the healing and skills development market in northwest Ohio, my business model will help navigate work/life balance and will further support cancer survivorship, all while exploring ways to extend the length of remission. Communities of cancer patients and survivors will access ways to heal one another while creating more networks and support groups. Advocacy for survivors will address the rapidly growing emphasis of legislative and economic concerns about Medicare regulations and the rising costs of healthcare benefits in the northwest Ohio marketplace. Using individualized coaching and career enhancement services, this program will be evaluated using a qualitative analysis method of focus groups and the evaluation of narrative and expressive writing. A low-cost seminar series will produce budding authors who are enthused about conducting community talks while facing potential unintended consequences or challenges.

I still choose to be a promise as a consultant in a growing industry of cancer survivorship—furthering my self-discovery and needing to know how to extend my period of remission, all while living a healthier and purpose-driven life of supporting other survivors.

I leaned in to my fears of being a cancer survivor, changed my relationships in Ohio, and finished my degree. I received an invitation to join the executive board of Cancer Connection of Northwest Ohio, co-authored a book, and starting a new business while operating three fundraisers that allowed me to cover startup costs and fund an upcoming three-week healing retreat. My life is calling me forth to think critically. I cannot think of a better place to be the cause in the matter of my life, than to return to college to complete a degree after so many years. It was the ultimate way to exercise my mental musculature while demonstrating self-love, self-worth and self-actualization.

I am loving with all my heart. My body is magically aligning with this power. There is no room for lack now that I am focused. God blessed my body and health. I am in total alignment and trust that nothing is by accident. I feel vertical and strong with every breath. I am expanding with love. My intention is to extend my period of remission by living a healthier, purpose-driven life as a subservient leader, an author, and an advocate for cancer survivors. Thank you for celebrating all cancer survivors and our continuous thirst for life. We are **Broken Crayons Still Coloring ...**

FINAL WORDS

We hope that you were empowered by the stories we have shared with you. We believe they have the ability to change your life. We are sure that while reading some of them you probably thought about your own story. Let's face it—we've all experienced a setback that positioned us for a comeback. This book is the final one in the *Delayed But Not Denied* anthology series. If you would like to participate with us on future projects, please contact us at **www.delayedbutnotdenied.info.**

Additionally, you may be interested in your own book anthology project for you and your tribe. If you would like us to assist you with creating a book compilation for you and your network, contact us. If you are interested in writing and publishing your own book, we can help there as well. Either way, you should contact us so we can discuss how we can assist you in making your author dreams come true. You can reach either Toni or Julia by emailing **admin@delayedbutnotdenied.info** or by calling us at **646-421-0830** or **917-501-6780.**

NOTES

NOTES

CPSIA information can be obtained
at www.ICGtesting.com
Printed in the USA
BVHW092148131118
533086BV00018B/181/P

9 781732 840522